THE NEW COMPLETE
irish wolfhound

On the site of the historic battlefield at Gettysburg, Pennsylvania, there stands a monument to stir the soul of every student of the American Revolution, every person whose roots reach to the green glens of Ireland, and every dog lover who has ever been awed by Cuchulainn, the great hound. This monument was erected in honor of the 63rd, 69th and 88th Regiments of New York—the Irish Brigade—and shows a stone effigy of an Irish Wolfhound in mournful aspect at the base of a Celtic cross. On page 99 of this book you will see a photo record of a visit to the Gettysburg monument by two present-day hounds—a blending of grace and beauty—past and present.

the new complete
irish wolfhound

Joel Samaha

HOWELL BOOK HOUSE

New York

Collier Macmillan Canada
Toronto

Maxwell Macmillan International
New York   Oxford   Singapore   Sydney

Howell Book House
Macmillan Publishing Company
866 Third Avenue, New York, NY 10022

Collier Macmillan Canada, Inc.
1200 Eglinton Avenue East, Suite 200
Don Mills, Ontario M3C 3N1

Library of Congress Cataloging-in-Publication Data
Samaha, Joel.
    The new complete Irish wolfhound / by Joel Samaha.
        p.   cm.
    ISBN 0-87605-171-9
    1. Irish wolfhound.   I. Title.
SF429.I85S26 1990
636.7′53—dc20   90-4288   CIP

Macmillan books are available at special discounts for bulk purchases for sales promotions, premiums, fund-raising, or educational use. For details, contact:

                    Special Sales Director
                    Macmillan Publishing Company
                    866 Third Avenue
                    New York, NY 10022

10 9 8 7 6 5 4 3 2

Printed in the United States of America

To

Mrs. Florence Nagle
Sulhamstead

and

Mrs. C. Groverman Ellis
Killybracken

Ch. Timber of Ambleside was a well-known winner and ambassador for the breed. He is shown here with his young master, Tommy Madigan, waiting out the long hours on the show bench. This portrait offers eloquent testimony to the inexhaustible well of Wolfhound patience.

Contents

The innate quality of the Irish Wolfhound's character has shown through its eyes for centuries. *Ludwig*

Foreword

THE INITIAL APPEARANCE of Alma J. Starbuck's *The Complete Irish Wolfhound* in 1963 marked a significant milestone in the long, romantic history of this splendid member of the purebred family. This truly definitive book became a classic in its own time and an essential part of any library of the Irish Wolfhound for novice and veteran fanciers alike.

It is in this illustrious tradition that *The New Complete Irish Wolfhound* now follows, not to replace the first book, but to bring the story of the great hound up to date and to give lovers of the breed an even deeper appreciation of all that makes the Irish Wolfhound so unique. Here again is the history of the breed to relish—a lore filled with fact, color, and maybe the contribution of an ancient *seannachie* (storyteller) or two to burnish the narrative. You decide which are the fairy tales. Here is a retelling of the tremendous contributions of Captain George Graham, and his dedication which resulted in the breed's being saved from almost certain extinction in the late nineteenth century and the heroic strides the legendary hound of Cuchulainn has made since his race was so dramatically snatched from oblivion.

Here also is what today's fancier should know about the hounds and their people that came before and established the tone found in the world of the Irish Wolfhound today. In the pages that follow, you will learn about the wise people that provided the good sense to keep this breed healthy and safe from exploitation. You will learn about the hounds that left their mark on the record books and on the pedigrees of generations that followed, and you will learn exactly what it means to share your home and your life with this benign giant that brought Romans to their feet, Vikings to their knees, and was the companion of kings and knights before Saint Patrick preached peace to the Hibernians.

Something else you will get from *The New Complete Irish Wolfhound* is a depth of understanding and appreciation of what the Irish Wolfhound is, both in spirit and in body. Here the Standard for the breed is presented and interpreted as a document to be lived with and used—the interpreter of true type in this time-honored hound.

Author Joel Samaha has all the credentials needed to bring forth a new, viable text on the breed. He is a veteran fancier who has owned Irish Wolfhounds in Great Britain and the United States. He has bred and actively shown his dogs against all comers and as a judge has brought his specialist's eye and educator's mind to the happy task of finding the best. He has been fortunate to learn from some of the breed's most revered authorities, and he now crystallizes these experiences for you in the book you now hold.

The New Complete Irish Wolfhound has the official approval of the Irish Wolfhound Club of America and is destined to mark a new milestone in the literature of the breed. As the Irish Wolfhound has been in the Howell breed book series for almost the entire history of the Company, we are especially honored and gratified to offer you this outstanding work. Furthermore, we are sure you will enjoy owning and learning from it as much as we have enjoyed bringing it to you.

Sean Frawley, President
Howell Book House
New York

the new complete
irish wolfhound

Marble statue found on the
Acropolis at Athens.

Man leading a hound before a pair-horse chariot. From a fresco at Tiryns.

1

Early History, Near Extinction, and Nineteenth-Century Restoration

"**Y**OU DON'T KNOW where you're going until you find out where you've been," history teachers are fond of telling their students. The history of the Irish Wolfhound demonstrates, with striking clarity, the truth of the history teacher's adage. For nearly three thousand years—as seen in the art from Greece and Cyprus reproduced here—a dog that combined power and speed has meant different things to different people. The thick neck and body on the hound atop the Acropolis clearly emphasizes power. In the hound running aside the ancient Cypriot's chariot, the accent is obviously on speed. The magnificent hound walking in front of the warrior in the fresco at Tiryns in the north of Greece illustrates what only a few great hounds have done throughout the ages: he combines power with speed, and is truly of "great size and commanding appearance."

THE IRISH WOLFHOUND IN ANTIQUITY

A hound of great size and commanding appearance, perfectly balancing speed and power in a Greyhound-like form has fascinated—and eluded—all who have loved the Irish Wolfhound. The Greek historian Arrian, writing in the second century A.D., mentions that the Celts had swift hounds when they sacked Delphi in 273 B.C. during the invasion of Greece. Statues, jewelry, and paintings bear witness to these large Greyhound-like dogs during the period. Phyllis Gardner's woodcut of the Tiryns fresco is another example that, according to Miss Gardner, accurately represents the ancient hound: Greyhound type, great size, weight, and power.

In 391 A.D., the Roman consul Quintus Aurelius Symmachus contributed seven "Irish dogs" to the Roman "Shows and Games," which "all Rome viewed with wonder." Irish Wolfhounds were valued and sought-after hunting dogs, not only because of their hunting prowess but also because they were exceptional guardians and companions. According to the chroniclers, as Cuchulainn, the bravest hero of the Irish in the first century, approached Culann the smith's house, Culann's "great hound" guardian set upon him. In the ensuing struggle, Cuchulainn slew the hound—no mean feat for a fifteen-year-old boy. Overcome with remorse, Cuchulainn offered to take the slain hound's place until he could train one of its pups.

Many ancient Irish chieftains and warriors called themselves Cu (Greyhound) or Mil-Chu (Greyhound that Hunts Large Game). According to Father Edmund Ignatius Hogan, S.J., the nineteenth-century historian of the breed, these appellations indicate how much the Irish loved, admired, and respected their Wolfhounds. Cuchulainn says of himself:

> I was a Greyhound (Cu) of catching deer,
> I was a Greyhound strong for combat,
> I was a Greyhound of visiting troops. . . .

During the third or fourth century, the poet Oisin celebrated the mythical mighty warrior and huntsman, Finn, son of Cumall. Finn was chief of the household of King Cormac, commander of the armies, and master of his hounds. His hounds supposedly numbered three hundred and his puppies two hundred. According to legend, when slipped, Finn's favorite hound, Conbec, could head off and bring back any stag in Ireland to Finn's main pack. It was said that no hound but Conbec did "ever sleep in the one bed with Finn." At

Traig Chonbicce, Finn's rival Goll drowned Conbec, after which Cailte, a warrior serving Finn, uttered the lay:

Piteous to me was Conbec's cruel death,
Conbec of perfect symmetry,
I have not seen a more expert of foot
In the wake of wild boar or stag.
A pang to me was Conbec's tragic fate,
Conbec of the hoarse deep voice;
Never have I seen one more expert of foot
At killing buck without delay,
A pang to me was Conbec's death,
Over the high, green billows,
His cruel death to me was a cause of strife,
His fate was most pitiful.

Another ancient story involved the Fianna, bands of Scots and Northern Britons who fought the Romans along Hadrian's Wall. They organized great hunts in which the chiefs, surrounded by their hounds, stood on commanding heights, while their followers with lesser dogs sought out and drove the game over a large area. When the chiefs sighted game, they slipped their hounds at it. Sometimes the hounds took as many as two hundred stags in one hunt.

THE IRISH WOLFHOUND IN MEDIEVAL TIMES

The English poet W. R. Spencer lauded King John's gift of an Irish Wolfhound to Llewellyn, Prince of Wales, in 1210.

The flower of all the race,
So true, so brave—a lamb at home,
A lion in the chase.
'Twas only at Llewellyn's board
The faithful Gelert fed.
He watched, he served, he cheered his lord,
And sentinelled his bed.
To sooth he was a peerless hound,
The gift of Royal John.

The ancient Irish Wolfhound also appears in the legends of other lands. The folklore of Iceland and other Scandinavian countries contains many references to the ancient hound. The great Spanish poet Lope de Vega, in his sonnet to the Irish Wolfhound, documents the Irish Wolfhound's presence in early Spanish history. Lope de Vega portrays a hound surrounded by an army of curs barking at him:

> This high-born Greyhound, without heeding them,
> Lifted his leg, wet the projecting angle of the wall,
> And through the midst of them went on quite at his ease.

ELIZABETHAN AND STUART HOUNDS

The great hunts of the Irish nobles and their Wolfhounds are the main focus of references to the breed from the twelfth to the sixteenth centuries. In 1571, thanks to Edmund Campion, S.J., we have the first detailed description of the form, size, and use of the Irish "Greyhound," as they were revealingly called then. While at Turvey, near Dublin, Father Campion wrote: "The Irish are not without wolves and Greyhounds to hunt them, bigger of bone and limb than a colt." Father Campion's name, Irish Greyhound, and his description remind us—as we must always remind ourselves—that the Irish Wolfhound is a large, powerful, *Greyhound*-like dog.

Father Hogan believed that the hounds Campion described were identical to the "big dogs of Ireland," "Greyhounds of Ireland," or "Wolfdogs of Ireland," sent as "highly prized presents to: Roman Consuls; to Kings of England, Scotland, France, Spain, Sweden, Denmark, and Poland; to Emperors, Great Moguls, Grand Turks, and the Shahs of Persia; to Ambassadors, Papal Nuncios, French Princes, and Dutch Noblemen; to Prime Ministers, Noblemen, and highborn beauties in Great Britain."

By the seventeenth century, few Irish Wolfhounds remained in Ireland. The disappearance of wolves and elk, and the steady depletion of the breed resulting from excessive exportation created so serious a shortage of Wolfhounds that a parliament sitting at Kilkenny in 1652 prohibited their further exportation. However, the Irish Wolfhound had not disappeared from England. Fredson T. Bowers, an American professor of English, respected judge, and brilliant scholar of our breed during the 1930s and 1940s, discovered a reference to the Irish Wolfhounds in England in a seventeenth-century play, William Wycherley's *The Gentleman Dancing Master*, published in 1672. In this play, a Spaniard and a Frenchman satirically describe each other. The Frenchman says to the Spaniard:

From Berwick's *Quadrupeds,* published in 1790. "The largest of the dog kind, and its appearance the most beautiful and majesic, about three feet high, generally of a white or cinnamon colour, and made somewhat like a Greyhound, but more robust; their aspect is mild, and their disposition gentle and peacable, their strength is so great that in combat the Mastiff or Bull Dog is far from being equal to them . . . . Next to this, in size and strength, is the Scottish Highland Greyhound or Wolf-Dog."

"And your Spanish hose, and your nose in the air, make you look like a great, grizzled, long Irish Greyhound reaching a crust from a high shelf, ha! ha! ha!"

Bowers says, in an important discussion of Irish Wolfhound type:

> This is one of the most fruitful references I have read in the past. It comes at a time when the hound has just about finished his work of exterminating the Irish wolves, and before the period of his decline has set in. Therefore, the date is a date when the hound is in his full flower and relative purity of blood, and should be close to the type of the traditional ancient breed. With these considerations in mind, now note the specific words. The hound is "great," that is, he is a huge hound, as he is today and has always been. This word is most frequently in the mouths of older writers of the breed.
>
> The next word is "grizzled." Without a doubt this word describes the various colored hairs which go to make up the peculiar characteristic of the hound's color which we know as "brindle." Probably Wycherley means also that the total effect is grey, as a person's hair is described as grizzled when its color is changing.
>
> The next word is "long," a singularly appropriate word to describe the rangy conformation of the Wolfhound, especially when he is stretching. This last detail is of the highest interest, for it is meant to emphasize the especial size and length of the dog, in short his great reaching ability, as the most vivid simile Wycherley could employ. Every detail confirms a dog of the characteristics known today, and all are peculiarly pertinent to the special qualities in the hound as we have him at the present time.

THE GEORGIAN IRISH WOLFHOUND

The Irish Wolfhound was not extinct in the eighteenth century, although it was no longer needed to help kings and nobles in the hunt. In 1770, Oliver Goldsmith wrote a revealing account in his *Animated Nature,* which, although written more than two centuries ago, bears quotation not only because it documents the state of the Irish Wolfhound in 1770, but also because it has much to teach us today.

> The last variety and most wonderful of all that I shall mention is the great Irish Wolfdog, that may be considered as the first of the canine species. This animal, which is very rare even in the only country in

the world where it is to be found, is rather kept for show than use, there being neither wolves nor any other formidable beasts of prey in Ireland that seem to require so powerful an antagonist.

The Wolfdog is, therefore, bred up in the houses of the great, or such gentlemen as choose to keep him as a curiosity, being neither good for hunting the hare, the fox, nor the stag, and equally unserviceable as a house dog. Nevertheless, he is extremely beautiful and majestic in appearance, being the greatest of the dog kind to be seen in the world. The largest of those I have seen, and I have seen above a dozen, was about four feet high, or as tall as a calf of a year old. *He was made extremely like a Greyhound, but rather more robust, and inclining to the figure of . . . the Great Dane* (emphasis added).

His eye was mild, his colour white, and his nature seemed heavy and phlegmatic. This I ascribe to his having been bred up to a size beyond his nature; for we see in man, and all other animals, that such as are overgrown are neither so vigorous nor alert as those of more moderate stature. The greatest pains have been taken to enlarge the breed, both by food and matching. This end was effectually obtained, indeed, for the size was enormous; but, as it seemed to me, at the expense of the animal's fierceness, vigilance, and sagacity. However, I was informed otherwise; the gentleman who bred them assuring me that . . . they would worry the strongest bulldogs in a few minutes to death. But this strength did not appear either in their figure or their inclinations; they seemed rather more timid than the ordinary race of dogs. . . . Whether with these disadvantages they were capable, as I was told, of singly coping with bears, others may determine; however, they have but few opportunities in their own country of exerting their strength, as all wild carnivorous animals there are only of the vermin kind. . . .

The Irish Wolfdog ears resemble those of the Greyhound, and are far from fluctuating with the animal's motions. But of whatever kind these dogs may be, whether known amongst the ancients, whether produced by a later mixture, they are now almost quite worn away, and only very rarely to be met with even in Ireland. If carried to other countries they soon degenerate, unless great care be taken, they quickly alter. They were once employed in clearing the island of wolves, which infested it in great plenty; but these being destroyed, the dogs also are wearing away, as if nature meant to blot out the species, when they had no longer any services to perform.

The early-nineteenth-century hound had little, if any, useful work to perform. Nevertheless, Philip Reinagle's hound appearing in the *Sportsman's Cabinet* in 1803 (and on this book's cover) was a grand dog. Reinagle, a member of the Royal Academy, depicted a spirited, gigantic, powerful Greyhound. The text accompanying the drawing reads:

> The Irish Greyhound is of an ancient race, is still to be found in some remote parts of the kingdom, though they are said to be reduced in size even in their original climate.

THE VICTORIAN IRISH WOLFHOUND

Grand the late Georgian hound may have been, but disquieting comments about "the last of the race" appeared increasingly. Only a few owners could still boast that their hounds contained one of three or four remaining strains of "genuine Irish Wolfdog blood." This did not discourage H. D. Richardson, who not only thoroughly researched the history of the Irish Wolfdog but also energetically worked to save it from extinction. In 1841, Richardson, in an illustrated article for an Irish journal, confidently asserted that despite claims to the contrary, the Irish Wolfdog still existed in Ireland. Richardson devotedly sought out all the remaining hounds he could find, bred from them, and eventually handed down the ancient strains to three stockmen who were equally committed to the preservation of the original hound: Sir John Power and Mr. Baker who carried on the Kilfane strain and later the Ballytobin, and Mr. Mahoney of Dromore. Mahoney's hounds did not survive—an all-too-common experience in breeding Irish Wolfhounds, as Captain Graham later discovered. Fortunately, Sir John Power and Mr. Baker successfully bred the Kilfane hounds from 1842 to 1873.

Mr. Baker did all he could to restore the breed to its original form. He went all over Ireland, acquiring the best remaining specimens no matter what he had to pay to get them. When he died in 1873, "he left a kennel of really fine dogs," according to Fredson T. Bowers.

CAPTAIN GRAHAM AND HIS WORK

Captain George Augustus Graham acquired the best of the hounds representing the Kilfane and Ballytobin strains that Mr. Baker left when he died. Graham revived the breed, beginning with

Reinagle's hound from *Sportsman's Cabinet,* 1803. "The Irish Greyhound is of an ancient race, is still to be found in some remote parts of the kingdom, though they are said to be reduced in size in their original climate." Captain Graham said about the Reinagle hound: "It is what the Irish Wolfhound was and should be."

a half-dozen of the Kilfane and Ballytobin stock. Graham vigorously pursued every extant hound claiming an authentic heritage to the ancient strains, judiciously outcrossed them to the Scottish Deerhound, and happily rehabilitated the breed. Captain Graham firmly believed that the Kilfane strain, descended from Richardson's hounds, preserved the ancient strains from extinction, trusting that Power and Baker had too much integrity to misrepresent their dogs' pedigrees. Furthermore, they had no financial or other personal interest in deception. Even if they had, other stock people could easily have discovered their fraud, and would surely have exposed it. Graham never bred into Lord Altamont's hounds, which line first Lord Derby and then Garnier continued.

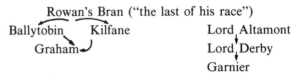

A "Manufactured" or Restored Breed?

Graham's many critics maintained that if an ancient Irish Wolfhound had ever existed, it was extinct. Therefore, the critics maintained, Graham and his predecessors had "manufactured" a new breed called the Irish Wolfhound by mixing Scottish Deerhounds, Great Danes, and Mastiffs. The criticisms stemmed in large part from nationalistic rivalries and antagonisms. The Irish discredited Graham's work because, although he was born in Scotland, he lived in England. To the Irish, nothing good could come from England. The Scots attacked Graham because he claimed the Scottish Deerhound descended from the Irish Wolfhound; the Scots could acknowledge no good coming from Ireland. The English deprecated Graham's work because they could see no good coming from either Ireland or Scotland! In 1885, Captain Graham responded to his critics:

> Though I by no means assert that we still have a pure strain, yet I distinctly contend and affirm that more or less true and authentic blood does exist—quite sufficient, indeed, whereon to rebuild the old breed, with the aid of analogous crosses, in its correct form. . . .

Crossing dogs in the nineteenth century was widely accepted because the breeds were not yet firmly defined nor had clubs acquired

The Irish Greyhound, from Bingley's *Memoirs of British Quadrupeds,* 1809.

Maida. Bred by Glengarry. Given to Sir Walter Scott in 1816.

a jealous and vested interest in maintaining breed purity. Breeders freely borrowed from any blood they believed could bring useful characteristics to their stock. Graham noted this practice:

> Excuse my so saying, but I hardly think the breed will be any more manufactured than has been the case with many that are now looked on as 'pure.' Recovered would strike me as a more appropriate term, and had it not been for this 'recovery' many of our best national breeds would have disappeared altogether, and believe me, Sir, it has not been accomplished without reverting freely to outside crosses.

Evidence abounds in sculpture, drawings, paintings, and written descriptions to support Captain Graham's belief that he and his predecessors had restored the ancient breed, not manufactured a new breed. This, of course, is not to doubt that Graham certainly used Deerhounds, which incidentally he did not consider a true cross because he believed that the Deerhound descended from the Irish Wolfdog. Other breeders most probably used the Great Dane because they needed size and power, qualities the remaining true specimens had lost. Graham himself never crossed a Deerhound and a Great Dane to "manufacture" an Irish Wolfhound, nor did he ever breed the offspring from such a cross. However, Great Dane blood probably existed in the backgrounds of his original stock, and later from crossing a Dane with the descendants of the true stock. Graham also resorted to one cross with a "heavy" Borzoi.

Mastiff blood mixed with the Irish Wolfdog from the earliest times. In 1797, the Earl of Altamount wrote:

> There were in Ireland two kinds of Wolfdogs—the Greyhound and the Mastiff. Till within these two years I was possessed of both kinds, perfectly distinct and easily known from each other. The heads were not sharp in the latter as in the former. . . . I have at present *five* Wolfdogs remaining, three males and two females; in these the two sorts appear to be mixed.

Altamont created a strain from these mixed Mastiffs and Greyhound Wolfdogs. His descendant, Lord Derby, carried on the strain after Altamont, and in Graham's time this strain still existed. According to Major Garnier, who procured the strain from Lord Derby, these hounds were massive, with coarse heads, flat coats, and large ears. Graham never bred from the Altamont hounds, but the coarse heads, flat ears, and other Mastiff characteristics that appear all too frequently in modern hounds clearly demonstrate that Mastiffs surely had their influence on the breed. This probably stemmed from the

Bitch with whelps, 1821.

The Irish Greyhound, from Brown's *Anecdotes,* 1829.

lack of purity throughout the breeds prior to and during Captain Graham's time.

The strains may not have been wholly pure—as no breed's then were—and Graham's predecessors, Graham, and his followers crossbred when necessary, but Graham's genius created in a few generations a uniformly typical powerful, rough-coated, galloping hound in a Greyhound-like form. Graham's dogs closely resembled the descriptions, sculptures, paintings, and other artwork that abounded, portraying the giant galloping Greyhound of proper type.

In the latter part of the nineteenth century, Father Hogan searched for references to Irish Wolfhounds and for evidence of their character, size, and appearance. In 1897, he published *The Irish Wolfdog,* of which all but a few copies were destroyed in a disastrous fire. Father Hogan could not get the book reprinted. Fortunately, ten years later, Joseph A. McAleenan of Long Island, a sportsman and lifelong friend of the dogs of Ireland, privately printed two hundred copies. Some were presented to McAleenan's friends; others found their way into libraries.

According to McAleenan, *The Irish Wolfdog,* "the only authoritative book on the subject, will excite interest and be the means of spreading an intimate knowledge of a dog that typifies the greatest in stature, intelligence, courage, loyalty, and affection of all the dog family." This *The Irish Wolfdog* surely does. It is a classic that anyone seriously interested in Irish Wolfhounds should read. It forms part of the culture of the Irish Wolfhound.

The Giant, Powerful, Greyhound-like Irish Wolfdog Type

Father Hogan's most important contribution is his painstaking search for references to Irish Wolfhounds from the time of ancient Rome to the late nineteenth century. In the nearly two hundred references to Irish Wolfhounds that Father Hogan reports, two inescapable conclusions follow: (1) that for nearly two thousand years, an amazing agreement as to proper Irish Wolfhound type has prevailed—Greyhound shape, in a large, *powerful* frame; and (2) that difficulty in maintaining the ideal balance between power and speed has always been the constant companion of those who breed Irish Wolfhounds. All who own, and especially those who breed and judge the hounds, must always remember those two signal conclusions.

Captain Graham's work clearly demonstrates Father Hogan's

The Irish Greyhound, from Blaine's *Encyclopedia of Rural Sports,* 1840; "... large and wiry coated... near three feet high... extremely mild in their disposition."

Nolan's Oscar and companion, 1841, from whom Captain Graham's dogs descended. Richardson said that Oscar was the finest specimen Richardson had ever seen. No hint of the Great Dane in this dog!

discoveries—the uniform agreement on Irish Wolfhound type, and the difficulty in breeding consistently for it. In 1862, Graham embarked on his daunting task of reviving the ancient breed; not until twenty years later had he succeeded in establishing the fragile beginnings of our modern dog. Listen to his own words on the challenges he faced:

> The writer has not only studied the subject carefully, but has bred extensively . . . though death and disease have hitherto robbed him of the finest specimens. Dogs have been bred approaching his ideal closely in looks, though wanting the required height and power; also dogs of very great height, &c, which were somewhat wanting in character. Yet the very certain knowledge has been gained from these efforts that it is perfectly possible to breed the correct type of dog.
>
> Several very fine dogs have been bred by the writer, but he has lost all the finest. He succeeded in rearing a remarkable dog that stood 33 inches, and was covered with a thick coat of nearly black shaggy hair. This dog most unfortunately died at seventeen months of age, leaving behind him one litter of puppies, of which few remain.

Graham's Stud Book entries for the early years amply demonstrate the challenges. A railway accident killed Sheelah, a bitch who carried the ancient strain into his day by a thread. Sheila had only one remaining son, a cryptorchid. Within the first few years, his Stud Book reports other cryptorchids and barren bitches. Graham faced a difficult choice: he could continue inbreeding and run the risk of total sterility, or crossbreed and further dilute the already dangerously weak original strains.

Captain Graham knew the dangers of inbreeding, not from the moral standpoint of incestuous relationships from which perspective some oppose it. Rather, he knew it as a stockman, unlike the rank novice or the ignorant breeder. In strong language, Captain Graham dealt with inbreeding:

> . . . no two dogs of the first cross should be mated together, as the produce will be certain to be most degenerate. The Foxhound, the Pointer, the Shorthairs, and many breeds of sheep and pigs have been brought to their present excellence by judicious outcrossing; why should not the same principle be applied to perfecting the Irish Wolfhound? *Too much in-and-in-breeding should be especially avoided, as size is thereby eventually lost to an alarming degree, even though character be retained* (emphasis added).

16

Irish Wolf Dog, drawn by W. R. Smith, 1843.

An oil on canvas owned by Mr. and Mrs. Frank Dean, Jr., signed and dated "L. O. Johnson, 1875."

The Precarious Balance of Irish Wolfhound Type

Fortunately, Captain Graham persevered with his judicious outcrossing and his avoidance of inbreeding; in doing so he saved the ancient breed from extinction. Graham's contributions did not stop with his breeding. He wrote the original Standard in 1885, a Standard based both on his exhaustive study of all old prints and historical references to the Wolfhound, his own firsthand experience with the Irish Wolfhound, and the knowledge of other stock people who knew the history and present state of the breed. The Irish Wolfhound Standard receives detailed attention in Chapters 5 and 6. The Standard constitutes the supreme authority in our efforts to breed the old Wolfdog to its fullest modern perfection.

The Standard that Graham and his fellow stock people created served them well; it also inspired and guided the great breed stalwarts who followed them right down to the 1980s. Those who now propose to tamper with their work should never forget this. A new Standard will not help us to preserve the ancient breed to its fullest perfection. Only true breeders who understand and apply the old Standard can accomplish this. In other words, we don't need a new Standard, we need breeders knowledgeable about animal husbandry in general and Irish Wolfhound type in particular.

Captain Graham possessed in abundance two indispensable qualities of the true breeder—patience and persistence. Concentrating first on size, he shortly turned to the greater and more daunting task—uniform type. The splendid O'Leary, whelped at the turn of the twentieth century, whose descendants constitute today's hounds, represents a triumph for Graham's work.

In 1885, the year the founders drafted the Standard, they also formed a club to preserve, protect, and promote the breed. Captain Graham never forgot the true type he was trying to produce. By repeatedly breeding back into the true strains, after judicious crossbreeding, he established the original strain's dominance. Graham surely possessed the first requisite in a breeding plan—to form an ideal; he obviously had in his mind's eye the image of the perfect dog he wanted to reproduce in living flesh. Miss Gardner credited Graham's breeding genius:

> The fact that Graham's strains bred true in remarkably few generations proves not only that he must have done his work very cleverly, but that the type he was working on was a definite and potent one.

18

Captain Graham

The founding of the Irish Wolfhound Club in 1885 paved the way for the breed's orderly growth in modern times. Members of the club promised to breed carefully and selectively from existing specimens only. The Dublin show in 1885 contained a class of twelve Irish Wolfhounds. For more than a century now—except for the war years—all principal championship shows in England and Ireland have had Irish Wolfhound classes.

The outstanding hounds bred during these formative years included Ch. O'Leary, the dog Captain Graham said breeders should study for type, and other notable hounds: Graham's own Ch. Sheelah, a ("very heavy bitch" and "very powerful," Graham's Stud Book entry reads); Brian II, a "rough-coated cream" with good hindquarters; and Cheevra, a powerful but, according to Graham, a "rather great-Daney" bitch who saved her breeder from a "savage pig."

CONSOLIDATION OF TYPE—1900–1950

Ch. O'Leary's death in 1892 marked a watershed. The breed's testing time had passed. Mrs. Starbuck reports that males particularly possessed proper size, and good conformation prevailed generally. By the 1920s, the founders had secured the modern hound, at least for the time being. Experience teaches, however, that breeders must remain ever vigilant against dilution of type. The breed was fortunate throughout the first two-thirds of the century to have a core of dedicated, experienced stock people to preserve and protect type. The challenge remains, as Goldsmith said in the eighteenth century, to retain an "extremely beautiful and majestic" dog, "made extremely like a Greyhound, but rather more robust," in a world where too many think of an Irish Wolfhound as a "curiosity."

I. W. Everett heads the list of early-twentieth-century breeders. He carried the breed through World War I, and his Felixstowe hounds were famous throughout the world. When he died in 1950, Mrs. Starbuck justly remarked that he left a legacy of work well done. The list of those active between World War I and World War II included a group of devoted, experienced breeders to whom we all a owe great debt. Their contributions, represented in their kennel names, appear in all present pedigrees. The list includes R. Montagu Scott—Ifold; Captain and Mrs. T. H. Hudson—Brabyns; Mrs. Barr—Grevel; Mrs. Florence Nagle—Sulhamstead; Miss M. S.

Captain Graham's Champion Sheelah, September 1882. From Graham's Stud Book: "Wolf-coloured. Hard coat. Very heavy bitch. 100-lbs. 27½ ins. (Massive, fawn or wolf colour. Wiry. Very powerful.)"

Cheevra, 1892, described in Graham's Stud Book: "Blue brindle. Poor coat. 28½ ins. Good bitch, rather Great Daney."

Kearns—Southwick; K. P. Strohmenger—Caval; Mr. D. le B. Bennett—Chulainn; Mrs. Beynon—Bournstream; Rev. C. H. Hildebrand—Clonard; Esther M. Croucher—Rippingdon; James V. Rank—Ouborough; Miss N. I. Nichols—Bradfield; Phyllis Gardner—Coolafin; Miss Ansel—Pentavalon; H. Pemberton—Comberfold; Mr. and Mrs. H. L. Crisp—Hindhead; H. R. Fisher—Lindley; Mr. T. B. Bolton—Steyning; Mrs. M. V. Massy—Wealdstone; E. G. Trousdale—Lynstone; Mrs. Knox—Raikeshill; and Dr. R. J. May—Ballytobin.

The late Mrs. Nagle, of Sulhamstead Kennels, breeder of nearly fifty English champions and innumerable champions in this country, described conditions during World War I:

I had my first Irish Wolfhound in 1913. I bred one litter during the First World War; at that time the Kennel Club would not register any pedigreed dogs except bred by their special permission, which was rarely given owing to the food position. In that litter was Sulhamstead Pedlar, who later made a real name as a sire. He sired Mr. Everett's unbeaten 37½ inch Ch. Felixstowe Kilcullen and was the grandsire of Sulhamstead Dan, exported to America, who became the ancestor of many famous American hounds. The line from Kilcullen was carried on by his brother, a large, very plain hound, Felixstowe Kilbarry, who sired Ch. Sulhamstead Conncara, out of Caragh, a great brood bitch, dam of Int. Ch. Sulhamstead Thelma, Ch. Acushla of Ouborough and Ch. Clodagh of Ouborough. These were all top class hounds.

Ch. Sulhamstead Conncara was one of the greatest sires in the breed, and his name is in nearly every Irish Wolfhound pedigree many times over. He had size, 36 in., quality and soundness of type. His was a romantic story, as he was born blind and his breeder Mrs. Lockhart was going to put him down but I had pick of the litter and went to see him and I thought he was the best Irish Wolfhound puppy I had ever seen, so I brought him home at six weeks old. He was blind but so outstanding I showed him and he got his title and nobody ever knew he was blind until I told them after he retired from the bench. He sired many great champions including Ch. Galleon of Ouborough and never produced a blind puppy.

During the last war very few Irish Wolfhounds were bred but the breed was just kept going, and just before that war I had another great dog, Ch. Sulhamstead Fella, who at ten months won the Challenge certificate and the Brewers Cup for the Best Hound at Birmingham. His sister Sulhamstead Fara was sent to America at the beginning of the war, became a champion and the dam of some great hounds.

Brian II, 1893, bred by Graham. Graham's Stud Book notes: "Cream-coloured. Rough. Long head, rather roman-nosed, long made, good limbs behind, and tail, but forelegs twisty. 135 lbs.? (Three pups only in this litter, the bitch dying young.)"

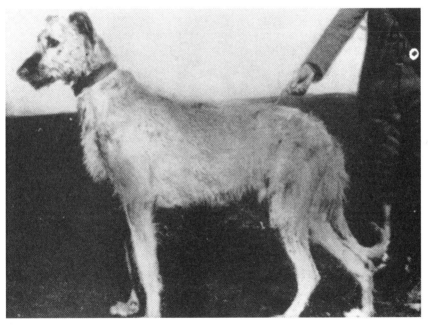

Ch. O'Leary, 1896, bred by Graham. Graham's Stud Book notes: "Crisp. 32½. Very good head. Good dog. Rather cow-hocked."

According to Esther Croucher, of Rippingdon Kennels, Ch. Sulhamstead Conncara and his descendant, Ch. Rippingdon Dan of Southwick, had more influence on the breed than any other Irish Wolfhounds. Along with two bitches, Hindhead Biddy of Ouborough and Sweetbriar of Rippingdon, these dogs appear somewhere in every present-day pedigree, if traced back far enough.

In reviewing the years from 1945 to the 1960s, Mrs. Nagle wrote:

> Things were now getting crucial, as every hound traced straight back to Clonboy of Ouborough and it was imperative to have an outcross. Thanks to the kindness of Miss Jeanette McGregor of America, who gave Rory of Kihone to the Irish Wolfhound Club, the situation was saved. Rory was selected by Miss Croucher during her visit to America as being suitable to mate with English bitches. She went for quality, conformation and soundness. . . . Many bitches came to Rory of Kihone, who revived the breed following the dearth of the World War II years.

All present-day owners and breeders owe our breed's existence to these experienced stock people who knew not only the principles of sound breeding in general but who also had firmly in their mind's eye that beautiful, powerful, large, rough-coated, Greyhound-like dog of ancient heritage.

Dr. May, Ballytobin Kennels, in his interesting *National Dog of Ireland,* tells a wonderful story that emphasizes the history of the Irish Wolfhound. When the British Expeditionary Forces evacuated the beaches at Dunkirk in June 1940, an Ulsterman soldier sighted an Irish Wolfhound straying on the sands. With his officer's permission, he and another Irishman took the hound to England. After the necessary quarantine, they took the hound to a military camp in County Antrim, where he became the regiment's mascot and the good friend of all the people in a nearby town. Every house in the neighborhood welcomed "Paddy."

> [Paddy's] history is bound up with the history of Ireland. He lived before history was born. He goes back to the mystic period of charmed romance, of legend, myth and fairy tale. His name is linked with round towers, ancient harps and shamrocks. He was the faithful companion and devoted friend of our Irish Saints (St. Patrick, St. Kevin and St. Brigid) as well as that of Kings, Warriors and Chieftains of Ireland.

Rajah of Kidnal, 1900, sired Ch. O'Leary. Graham's Stud Book notes: "Light brindle. 32-ins. Lengthy forelegs and feet poor. Good mover. Moderate bones. . . . Presented to the Irish Guards in 1902."

Tynagh, 1899, according to Graham's notes, "31 ins. Grey brindled. Good head ["snipey" erased], strong. Good in many ways. Curved bone front legs, heroine of Dawson's book, *Finn the Wolfhound.*"

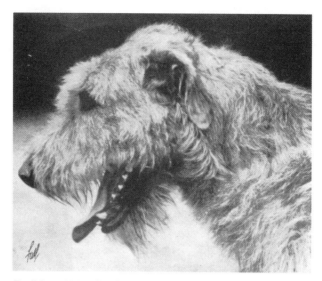

English and Irish Ch. Galleon of Ouborough, a successful show dog and sire in England during the late 1920s and early 1930s.
Thomas Fall

English Ch. Rippingdon Rathgelert.   *C. M. Cooke*

Joseph A. McAleenan, advising Walter A. Dyer, who was about to write a "new" article on the breed in 1920, had some harsh words for those who write about the Irish Wolfhound's history: "I hope you are not going to write of the dog of past centuries. Write of the present dog. The field is large enough and the breed holds an interest that is purely modern. The old Irish dog has had his day. . . ." Of course, we live in the present; hence, we should not dwell unduly on the past. However, we must give our knowledge of history its due: we can hardly know where we are, or where we are going, unless we know where we have been.

Hopefully, this brief history of the Irish Wolfhound will help all breeders, owners, and judges to keep in mind the true description of the Irish Wolfhound—a beautiful, powerful, rough-coated, Greyhound-like dog of great size and commanding appearance, fleet enough to catch a wolf and sufficiently powerful to bring it down. A hound, Mrs. Nagle said, that "I would like to have by my side if I should ever encounter a wolf." The appreciation of type should inspire breeders to meet the challenges Graham encountered and to pursue the course so that we can pass along the great heritage the breed stalwarts happily gave to us in the form of the Irish Wolfhound.

Early Days at Halcyon Farms, circa 1929. To the left of Mrs. E. T. Clark is Ch. Felixstowe Kilgarth. To the right is Ch. Felixstowe Kilbagie. In front are Felixstowe Kilmichael, Princess of Coval, and Chulainn Dantless.

2

The Irish Wolfhound Comes to America

In 1838, Henry Hastings Sibley, first governor of Minnesota, imported a pair of Irish Wolfhounds from England, the first recorded in America. "Tiger" and "Lion" were much larger and heavier than Deerhounds, although "equally fleet," according to Father Hogan. A portrait of Lion still hangs in the Sibley mansion in St. Paul. Lion resembles Reinagle's painting, and more closely fits Goldsmith's description—"made extremely like a Greyhound, but rather more robust"—than the short-coupled, low-to-the-ground hounds sadly seen all too often today.

Father Hogan also refers to an apparently no-longer-extant stuffed, rough-coated white Irish Wolfhound in a Minneapolis museum. In 1892, Father Hogan mentions an Irish Wolfhound that reputedly killed forty wolves in the Rocky Mountains. Joseph Coll, an early member of the Irish Wolfhound Club of America, said his father brought an Irish Wolfhound to Philadelphia when he immigrated from Ireland in the 1850s. In 1879, Bevis, imported from Ireland, appeared in the Westminster Kennel Club Show, becoming the first documented Irish Wolfhound exhibited in an American dog show. According to the *American Kennel Club Gazette,* Bevis was "an Irish Wolfhound of the highest class." A bit short and square in muzzle, Bevis is portrayed in an 1880 lithograph as a powerful hound, perhaps not the ideal Greyhound type.

During the early years, General Roger D. Williams of Lexington, Kentucky, registered approximately 125 Irish Wolfhounds under his Rockwood Kennels prefix, perhaps the first Irish Wolfhound kennel in America. Mrs. Norwood B. Smith, founder and first president of the Irish Wolfhound Club of America, first saw Irish Wolfhounds in 1915, and later recalled that they "were all I imagined Irish Wolfhounds to be, and then some." In 1921, Mrs. Smith launched her famous Cragwood Kennels, from which she bred some of the leading hounds in America. The Cragwood hounds represented the true Greyhound-like dog, combining power and speed. Five years later, in 1926, Mrs. L. O. (Alma) Starbuck established the famous Ambleside Kennels, which during its period of activity registered more than 500 Irish Wolfhounds.

THE GOLDEN AGE

The Golden Age of American Irish Wolfhounds followed. Enthusiastic, dedicated, knowledgeable stock people imported the best English bloodlines and bred selectively from them. Halcyon Kennels, led by the Edward T. Clarks, were leading importers and breeders. So, too, was the late Mrs. C. Groverman Ellis, whose Killybracken Kennels imported and produced many top-winning hounds. Mrs. Ellis was more than a breeder. She opened her house, her heart, and her mind to all who wanted to listen. She taught more than how to breed dogs; she taught how to own them, how to treat them, and how to exhibit them. More than that, she taught us the nature of sportsmanship. Such phrases as "My father said, 'If you can't say something nice, then don't say anything" and "I take the dog I admire and hope the judge agrees; if not, well then I'll come another day" were more than precepts; they reflected the way Mrs. Ellis lived her life. If novices to the breed learn nothing more than these two lessons, they will have learned a great deal.

In the fall of 1926, the American Kennel Club held a "model" show during the Sesquicentennial in Philadelphia. Mrs. Smith contacted all new Irish Wolfhound owners, as well as longtime owners, urging them all to show their hounds at the Sesquicentennial show. The AKC provided only two classes not divided by sex for the fourteen Wolfhounds entered. According to Mrs. Starbuck, this pro-

Ch. Felixstowe Kilmorac Halcyon, the second Irish Wolfhound to win a Best in Show in the United States. *Rudolph W. Tauskey*

Ch. Halcyon Allanah of Ambleside, a Specialty and Westminster winner in the late 1930s. *Rudolph W. Tauskey*

voked Mrs. Smith to gather a group of Irish Wolfhounds to determine how best to both promote the breed's interests and acquaint the public with their grand qualities. The group met, formed a club, and applied for membership in the American Kennel Club.

THE IRISH WOLFHOUND CLUB OF AMERICA (IWCA)

The Irish Wolfhound Club of America (IWCA) held its first meeting the following year at Westminster, where the group benched sixteen Irish Wolfhounds. The founding members included two whose kennels have made a major contribution to the Irish Wolfhound in twentieth-century America: Mrs. Norwood B. Smith, Cragwood Kennels, and Alma O. Starbuck, Ambleside Kennels. The IWCA organized itself along the English Club's pattern and adopted the English standard for the breed.

Mrs. Smith wrote the first "President's Message," a practice that every IWCA president has followed. In the first edition of *The Complete Irish Wolfhound,* this book's predecessor, Mrs. Starbuck included Mrs. Smith's message; in 1969, when the book entered its third edition, Samuel Evans Ewing III, Eagle Kennels, and Rosalie Graham, Cu Kennels, still thought the message deserved repeating. With minor alterations, I include it too, not only as a piece of history, but also because it remains fully relevant in the 1990s.

The Irish Wolfhound has improved much within the last ten years. Our judges are coming more and more to demand soundness. The time was when a St. Bernard won by his head, so it seemed, and it was suggested that some of the exhibitors provide themselves with wheelbarrows to bring in the rear of their dogs. How much more important that the Irish Wolfhound, a sporting breed, should be sound and able to move with ease and grace. *Soundness and a conformation suitable to its purpose in life is one of the prime requisites of all breeds.*

Size is intriguing. The untrained eye can recognize and appreciate bigness, a beautiful color and fine coat, just as all register pleasure in hearing a simple musical air. To catch all the nuances in a great masterpiece the ear must have received technical training. This is the recognition of quality, and the lack of ability to define quality is the reason that so often those along the side lines cannot follow the judging. We must guard against catering to the applause of the gallery

Club meeting at Halcyon Farms after second Specialty.

Framingham Kennel Club Show, August 1940. Judge, Mr. Eskrigge.

33

Ch. Roonagh of Ambleside, whelped February 1931. By Sulhamstead Dan ex Ch. Kathleen of Ambleside. Best of Opposite Sex, 1934 Specialty; Winners Bitch, Westminster, 1933 and 1935; Best of Breed, Westminster, 1936.

Rathmullan Kennels' Ch. Balbricken of Ambleside. Best in show, all breeds, four times in 1934 and once in 1935.

Ch. Gillagain of Ambleside, owned by Paul Paine, was an all-breed Best in Show winner in 1946.

The sisters Ch. Laith of Kihone (foreground), Best of Opposite Sex at the 1949 IWCA Specialty and Spaglainn of Kihone. Both were bred and owned by F. Jeannette McGregor of Kihone Kennels.

and being content if we merely produce a huge, spectacular hound. Our Irish Wolfhound belong in the classical, not the jazz class. He is more than just the largest breed of dog, he is the greatest. Many of our hounds now measure thirty-six inches and over and weigh one hundred and fifty pounds at one year. I doubt if the breed can with safety stand more size unless by some miracle we can lengthen the growing period. As it now is, Jack's Bean Stalk is the only thing that has the edge on him.

Points to be stressed are shoulders, stifles, back line, and hocks. No horse or dog with a straight shoulder can really run. The straight shoulder belongs to the draught animal. Let us watch our stifles that they are well bent, giving a graceful sweep to the hind legs and enabling the dog to push himself along when running instead of just pounding the ground. The back must arch to act as a sort of spring which recoils with every bound. The loin furnishes the motive power for driving the hind legs, so must be broad and strong. The lung cavity must be large but not too wide.

Given this big, useful frame we may turn our attention to ears, which sadly need "fixing." We meet all sorts of ears. Three quarters of them are wrong. The Standard is quite clear on the subject. They should be small and folded like a Greyhound's. Many of our hounds, when relaxed, carry them Dane fashion. Eyes over here as a rule are good. The coat seems to vary from the almost smooth coat to something akin to the Old English Sheepdog. Whatever its length, it should be coarse. A fine, silky, or fuzzy coat is an abomination, as it soaks up water, and all sorts of burrs stick to it. Brows, eyelashes and whiskers are necessary to impart the true Irish expression and these should adorn a long, rather lean head with plenty before the eyes and showing great strength at the end of the muzzle.

IWCA SPECIALTIES

At its first meeting, the IWCA agreed to support two shows each year: Westminster, held at Madison Square Garden in New York City, and a "Specialty," preferably an outdoor show. The original plan, according to Mrs. Starbuck, was "fun while it lasted." However, it created "complex judging problems that arise when we are sponsoring classes at an all-breed show and calling it 'Our Specialty.' " The Club soon started holding a separate Specialty show, now a firmly established annual spring event.

Exhibitors travel great distances, at great expense, to these Specialties. The National Specialty—and now several Regional Spe-

Ch. Felixstowe Kilgarth, Winners Dog at the 1929 Specialty.

cialties—provide the opportunity both for serious breeders, spectators, breeder judges, all-rounders, from here and abroad, to assess the state of the Irish Wolfhound annually. Now a three-day event drawing entries exceeding five hundred dogs, the IWCA holds its National Specialty variously in the East, the Midwest, the Central states, the Southeast, and the West.

3

The Modern Irish Wolfhound: From the Golden Age to the Present

T HE STATE of the Irish Wolfhound world during the 1950s reflected the times in general. The era of "gracious living" was not yet over, President Eisenhower made people "feel good" about themselves and their country, the economy was apparently sound, and the country turned from great social experiments to more private and personal fulfillment. The closely knit, personal world of Irish Wolfhounds all seemed solid and secure—with good reason. Several of the breed's founders remained active, providing added stability and security in an already relatively stable and secure period. The founders of the breed in America still dominated the scene in the 1950s. Mrs. Smith, the oldest breeder in America, and her Cragwood Kennels remained an important force. L. O. Starbuck had died, but Mrs. Starbuck carried on Ambleside Kennels in California in partnership with Colonel William D. Dana on his ideal ranch. Mrs. Ellis, sportswoman *par excellence,* provided all owners with a model example, and her Killybracken Kennels produced many winners. Her Barn Hill Dan Malone became the first Irish Wolfhound in America to win a Best in Show at an all-breed dog show—Stone City Kennel Club, 1950. Mrs. Dot Wofford's Rathrahilly Kennels in Kansas is still known today through her daughter Mrs. Paul Seymour, Jr., who has devotedly carried on the Rathrahilly line.

THE PLACID 1950s

Names "new" in the 1950s, but well known today because of their present activities, also appeared. Samuel E. Ewing III, whose Eagle Kennels have produced innumerable champions, finished his first champion in 1957—Ch. Ballymacad of Ambleside. General Alfred W. de Quoy, Keltic Kennels, whose erudite works on Irish Wolfhounds include *The Irish Wolfhound Guide, Registrations 1956–1964,* and *The Irish Wolfhound in Irish Literature and Law,* quickly became known as a "statistics star." He also emphasized the Irish Wolfhound in Obedience.

This core of founders and "new" people—fewer than fifty families—continued to develop the breed, expand membership in the Irish Wolfhound Club of America and in the regional clubs, and encourage entering Irish Wolfhounds at all-breed and specialty shows. The few active breeders were "stock people." They brought their interest and knowledge of animal husbandry in general to bear on the breeding and care of Irish Wolfhounds. These experienced breeders and their protégés registered approximately one hundred hounds annually. They had not only the experience, but also the leisure and resources to take the responsibility of breeding seriously. Imported hounds from leading English and Irish Kennels—Sulhamstead, Boroughbury, Brabyns, and Ballykelly—periodically infused domestic bloodlines with new blood.

Specialties were "intimate affairs" during the Golden Age of Irish Wolfhounds. From 1953 to 1962, Amory Haskell—according to *Harp and Hound,* "a member from the early days of the Club's founding . . . staunch admirer and supporter of the breed"—hosted the annual event at Woodland Farm, his New Jersey residence. Miss F. Jeanette McGregor, Kihone Kennels, IWCA president, captured much of the feeling and atmosphere of the Golden Age of Irish Wolfhounds in America when she paid tribute to Mr. Haskell's contributions to the breed:

Ch. Tralee of Ambleside, owned by Charles H. Morse, Jr., won two all-breed Bests in Show in 1954 and one in 1955. He was also Best of Breed at the IWCA Specialty in 1954, 1955, and 1956 and was Best at the West Coast Specialty in 1952; Hound of the Year, 1954 and 1955.

Ch. Barn Hill Dan Malone, owned by Killybracken Kennels, was an all-breed Best in Show winner. He is shown here with Mrs. C. Groverman Ellis following a Hound Group first at the Rock River Valley KC show in 1950.

Over the years he and his family have offered their help and support to the Irish Wolfhound Club in many and various ways, such as his gracious welcome and his unstinting hospitality to members at his home, Woodland Farm, for our Specialty show and annual meeting for the past ten years.

It was at Woodland Farm that our largest entries have been attained, first under the judging of our fellow member, Mrs. Florence Nagle of Sussex, England, who flew to the United States especially for our show, then later under Mrs. Geraldine R. Dodge, of Madison, New Jersey, one of the first ladies of American dogdom, and lastly under another fellow member, Walter Reeves. . . . The ten years at Woodland Farm will be rightly known as the "Golden Era."

Harp and Hound's editor, Gordon Graham, noted that

the specialties at Woodland Farm drew record entries, attracting the breeders and owners of many of the best Irish Wolfhounds in the country. Interest in and improvement of the breed were stimulated far more than would have been possible otherwise.

Some of the decade's leading events illustrate the combination of continuity and gradual change in the breed and its custodians. In 1950, Ambleside Kennels celebrated its Silver Anniversary. Tom Wanamaker's Brian Boru of Edgecliff (Ch. Arnold of Edgecliff ex Tara of Ouborough) won *three* Hound Groups in 1950, a monumental win for that decade. Esther Croucher, Rippingdon Kennels, traveled twelve thousand miles by boat and rail to Long Beach, California, in 1951 to judge the first National Specialty ever held in the West. The following year, Mrs. Smith, one of America's most senior breeders, won Best of Breed with her homebred Cragwood Barney O'Shea (Cragwood Gaelic Harp ex Barn Hill Gilda) in the largest American Specialty in history—forty-three hounds! Miss F. Jeanette McGregor exported her Rory of Kihone (Taddeus of Kihone ex Chalet Cam) to England, the only American dog ever to become an English champion. According to Miss Croucher, Rory possessed "perfect type," appeared in every English pedigree, and "pulled the breed up just in time to save it from . . . fatal faults" brought on by the crisis created when the English had to largely forgo breeding during World War II.

In 1956, Ch. Tralee of Ambleside, "a big bitch of the most desirable type and who moves so wonderfully she leaves you breathless," (Alva Rosenberg, all-breed judge, said after awarding Tralee Best of Breed at the 1955 Specialty) became the first Irish Wolfhound ever to win three Specialties. She retained that record until Ch. Wild

Alma J. Starbuck, the Mistress of Ambleside, exerted a profound influence on the Irish Wolfhound in America. Her hounds were known and appreciated from coast to coast even when travel with dogs, especially giant breeds, was a difficult undertaking. She is shown here taking a win with a young hound under judge Anton Korbel at the old Harbor Cities (California) KC show. *Joan Ludwig*

Mona Craig of Ambleside, shown scoring Winners Bitch at the 1953 IWCA Specialty under the veteran authority Walter H. Reeves. The handler here is Mary Jane Ellis. *William Brown*

Isle Warlock broke that record in 1979, when Mrs. Bregy, his breeder, owner, and handler, took him to a fourth Specialty win. Another first closed the Golden Age. Mrs. Nagle awarded two littermates Best of Breed and Best of Opposite Sex at the 1959 Specialty: Ch. Brogan and Ch. Brickeen of Hillaway. Their breeder-owner-handlers were Misses Helen Dalton and Catherine Cram of Maple Plain, Minnesota, whose Hillaway Kennels provided spacious quarters for the hounds and who offered gracious hospitality, kindness, and help to all who admired Irish Wolfhounds.

THE TURBULENT 1960s

The 1960s opened with promise and optimism, in the world at large and in the smaller world of Irish Wolfhounds as well. When the Irish Wolfhound Club of America honored Amory Haskell for his devotion, support, and hospitality to the breed in 1963, Miss McGregor confidently maintained that the breed was still in its Golden Age. However, the turmoil of the middle and late years of that decade in the country at large also had its counterpart in uncertainties in the world of Irish Wolfhounds. These uncertainties stemmed in some measure from the same source—a burgeoning, young, restless population flush with affluence and leisure, looking to do something with their time and money. Owning, showing, and breeding Irish Wolfhounds was no longer the preserve of a relatively small number of families who had lived with Irish Wolfhounds for many years. More and more "new faces" came, and sadly "went," within the space of a few years or even less. Showing was no longer an intimate affair. Increasingly, exhibitors did not know their fellow exhibitors and sometimes did not recognize the names and pedigrees of the dogs who appeared at dog shows.

Breeding ceased to be solely the province of a few experienced "stock people" steeped in the knowledge of animal husbandry. Increasingly, owners with little or no experience, either of livestock in general or of Irish Wolfhounds in particular, bred their hounds, sometimes "for the fun of it," sometimes because they found it an "intellectual" challenge to work with genetics they had learned from books, and most often because it was the era of "do your own thing." Lessening respect for authority, for tradition, and unfortunately for experience and knowledge, led too many people in general and Wolf-

Ch. Arnold of Edgecliff, an all-breed Best in Show winner in 1949, owned by Edgecliff Kennels. *Joan Ludwig*

A group of yearlings from 1956—the "Hounds of Hillaway"—owned by the Misses Helen Dalton and Catherine Cram, waiting their turn in the ring.

Ch. Lacey of Ambleside, Best of Opposite Sex at the West Coast Specialty in 1957 and Best of Breed at the same Specialty in 1958, owned by Alma J. Starbuck. *Joan Ludwig*

hound owners in particular to conclude that everyone had the capacity to do anything.

However, all Irish Wolfhound owners, who concededly had a *legal* right to become breeders, and who in fact did so simply by putting a bitch they owned to an available dog, could not by virtue of that alone possibly appreciate, comprehend, or properly bear the custodial responsibility for the future of the Irish Wolfhound. The challenge remained to breed—and to leave for the future—a large rough-coated, Greyhound-like dog that combined the speed to overtake a wolf and the power to bring him down, a majestic hound of great size and commanding appearance. The challenge required recruiting, teaching, and serving a larger, more diverse, energetic, eager, and restless group of owners who would appreciate the heritage and complexities of, and accept the responsibilities attendant upon, caring for our breed.

Increasing numbers signify the single most important fact about Irish Wolfhounds during the 1960s. The number of Irish Wolfhounds expanded; the number of people who owned them increased; and the number of *novice* breeders grew. Some attributed the rise in numbers to the gift of an Irish Wolfhound puppy to President Kennedy shortly before his assassination in 1963. The Irish breeder publicized the gift, and the American press covered the story, showing President Kennedy and his family receiving the puppy at the White House. The Kennedys quietly asked the IWCA to find the puppy a good home, so it never lived with them.

The causes for the population increase were a good bit more complex than this incident can account for, although clearly it brought Irish Wolfhounds more into public view. Despite the increase, the numbers were not out of control, were, in fact, nothing like the explosive increases during the 1970s and 1980s. The entries at the IWCA Specialty did not exceed 100 until 1960. The number of active breeders reached 184 in the same year, and although many new names appeared, many old established names, and particularly families, remained. Nevertheless, the numbers rising on all fronts, combined with the temper of the 1960s generally, had their effects.

Perhaps the most serious consequence of the rising numbers in general, and particularly the growth in inexperienced breeders, was that they led to what would become clearly a crisis in the uniformity of type by the 1970s. As early as 1962, the veteran all-rounder Walter Reeves, who had sixty years of experience observing Irish Wolfhounds, sounded one of the earliest warnings. He had found a typical "stallion hound," Celeste Hutton's Ch. Greysarge Cristel's Corrigan, whom he awarded Best of Breed at the Irish Wolfhound Club of America Specialty in 1962. Nevertheless, he noted a disturbing characteristic of the entry overall—the dilution of uniform type. He commented upon it in his after-dinner remarks following the Specialty. Later, in writing to *Harp and Hound,* the official publication of the Irish Wolfhound Club of America, he called upon the IWCA and its members to do something about the problem:

> I hope the members of the Club were not offended at what I said about type after the dinner. I realize I am not a breeder, only an honorary member, but I know of no other breed today that has such distinct types competing. This is most confusing to the judges and I humbly suggest to the members of the Irish Wolfhound Club that the time has come for them to decide which type they wish the judge to consider as the correct Irish Wolfhound.

Of course, preserving type was not a challenge unique to the 1960s. Throughout the history of the breed, observers have noted the variety of types, particularly the broad differences between the Mastiff-type dog and the galloping hounds that resembled the Greyhound. However, beginning with Captain Graham in England, a small core of breeders on both sides of the Atlantic established the Wolfhound type. As the numbers of owners, hounds, and active breeders increased, and spread across the continent, control over type loosened.

More breeders knew less about general animal husbandry or the history of the Irish Wolfhound and were less subject to the influence of those who did. Unknown to most inexperienced breeders, Captain Graham restored the ancient Irish Wolfdog—the more robust, large, Greyhound-like dog—by carefully blending the old true Irish Wolfdog with equally carefully selected crossbred animals. True Irish Wolfhound type remained fragile, hence susceptible to easy corruption and dispersal. The care and expertise in retaining, not to mention fortifying, breed type called for knowledge and experience that novice Irish Wolfhound breeders, and even breeders not highly educated about Irish Wolfhound history and breeding did not—and still do not—possess.

A second consequence of rising numbers was the appearance of profit-seeking opportunists. References began to appear, occasionally at first, but then more frequently, to imported litters, to Irish Wolfhounds available from commercial sources, and to breeders interested mainly in turning a profit. Commercialism may not be all bad. In fact, the history of the breed, particularly in England, has

48

Ch. Sulhamstead Matador of Killybracken, owned by Killybracken Kennels, was the winner of nine Bests in Show in 1958. He is shown here being awarded Best of Breed at the IWCA Specialty in 1960 under judge Louis J. Murr; he was handled by his owner Mrs. C. Groverman Ellis. The trophy presenter is F. Jeannette McGregor.   *William Brown*

Ch. Greysarge Cristel's Corrigan (Int. Ch. Castledawn Tartan ex Ch. Cristel of Ambleside), owned and bred by Celeste Winans Hutton, was Best of Breed at the IWCA Specialty in 1961 under judge Mrs. Geraldine R. Dodge. Corrigan was handled by his owner to this good win and the trophy was presented by Miss F. Jeannette McGregor.
William Brown

included breeders who needed to make a profit in order to stay active. But these breeders, at least most of them, were steeped in the knowledge of the breed and in livestock management generally. Mrs. Nagle, in commenting on the commercial breeders of earlier times, pointed out that the need for money, combined with their knowledge, experience, and interest in the breed, actually *enhanced* the quality of their stock. The prod of profit, coupled with the need to survive, led early commercial breeders to breed typical hounds, because the select few who wanted Irish Wolfhounds demanded typical hounds. The satisifed owners, the successful show records under knowledgeable judges, and the high quality of these commercial breeders' stock raised the demand for hounds of quality.

The combination of experience, knowledge, interest in the breed, *and* the need for money rarely appears in any age, and never among the profit seekers witnessed in America beginning in the 1960s. Fortunately, most commercial breeders found that Irish Wolfhounds of low quality, poor health, and questionable background do not "sell." Unfortunately, this recognition did not occur in some cases until individual hounds suffered, sometimes unspeakably, from the consequences of "businesses" in trouble, whose owners cut their losses at the dogs' expense. Dogs suffered not only from these "proprietors' " ignorance, but also from their calculated greed.

Poor sportsmanship, bad manners, and just plain ignorance about showing dogs also began to surface, particularly during the late 1960s. Fredson Bowers, the erudite, experienced Wolfhound owner and judge, felt the need to comment about a satellite show following the 1966 Specialty:

> If one is interested enough to show [his Wolfhound] one should be concerned to keep him in training. A patient judge may be willing to waste time to do justice to the dog, despite the dog's and owner's best efforts to hide any virtues the dog may have possessed.

Furthermore, he added another point, one today's spectators should take to heart:

> It is interesting and proper for those watching to comment—but they should choose seats removed from the earshot of the judge.

Always the shrewd observer, Rosalie Fox, commenting later, noted:

> And this was mild enough rebuke for the bad manners that marred a special day for Irish Wolfhounds. The "comments" referred to were very partisan and were directed at the judge.

Despite these negative consequences of rising numbers, breed affairs retained a distinctly personal quality, in large part because devoted old-time breeders and owners were determined to keep them that way. Individuals and their spouses hosted all the Specialties on their private grounds, despite the increasing difficulty that greater numbers posed in order to do so. Amory Haskell hosted the first three Specialties of the decade; then the Weavers offered their Glengyle Farms for 1964 and 1965. Gordon and Rosalie Graham (later Mrs. Kelly Fox) hosted the 1966 and 1967 Specialties at their Shadow Hill residence on Long Island; the event was held at "Dot" Wofford's Rimrock Farm near Wichita, Kansas, in 1968 and at the Barclay Morrisons' Redgate in 1969 and 1970.

Perhaps nothing reveals the intense desire on the part of the most experienced breeders and owners to retain the personal element in an increasingly impersonal, scattered, and growing world of Irish Wolfhounds than the following letter written by a grateful novice about Mrs. Ellis.

> I would like to say a few things about Mrs. Ellis, including the fact that she knows absolutely nothing about this letter. Shortly after I obtained my Irish Wolfhound I contacted Mrs. Ellis and began asking questions. I must have asked 500 questions both by phone, and by her invitation at her home. She even looked my Irish Wolfhound over and gave me what I consider to be an expert's appraisal of the dog's quality. Suffice to say she was, and is, simply marvelous. She took her valuable time and knowledge and freely gave it to a perfect stranger who is not a member of the IWCA, who doesn't yet subscribe to *Harp and Hound*, and who didn't even buy his dog from her.
>
> Thanks in large measure to Mrs. Ellis my Irish Wolfhound is thriving. If she is typical of Irish Wolfhound breeders and fanciers as a whole, then as a new Irish Wolfhound fancier, but a long time dog lover, I would say that other breeds would do well to seek some new blood. (Robert L. Stevenson, Concord, N.H.)

Mrs. Ellis—and others like her—worked tirelessly to combat ignorance, to educate the novices, and to welcome them into the world of Irish Wolfhounds. The IWCA also made an organized effort to join in educating and welcoming new owners. The Club published a booklet prepared to meet the novices' demands for information about Irish Wolfhounds—where to find them, how to rear them, what to feed them, and all too often, how to breed them.

Sportsmanship, so vital to showing Irish Wolfhounds, and one hallmark of the intimacy and camaraderie of the early Golden Age, happily continued to prevail, at least during the early and mid-1960s. Rosalie Fox reports the following remarkable incident, one that *all* of us—old, young, new, and old—should have indelibly imprinted in our memories:

> Anyone present at one particular Specialty in the early sixties will recall an inadvertent miscarriage of judgment and the sportsmanlike way the circumstances were understandingly and gracefully accepted: A very elderly and respected gentleman, exhausted by the rigors of the day, judged several of the final classes seated beside the judge's table. He had already awarded Greysarge Cristel's Corrigan Best of Breed (it was Corrigan's second in a row) when the stud dog class entered the ring. Corrigan followed his sire, Ch. Castledown Tartan, in for the class. Tartan, 8 years old, had been relieved of some of his tail several years before, due to an injury, and properly the ring steward was so informed. From his chair, the judge sent the steward to excuse Tartan and his get from the ring. Tartan had won this class with the same abbreviated tail the previous year when Mrs. Dodge had judged. Celeste [Hutton] matter-of-factly accepted the patently unfair dismissal, was on hand to congratulate the winner, and the incident passed, unremarked.

Exhibitors today could also learn from an incident involving Mrs. Nagle, Sulhamstead Kennels. Confronted with poor judging in one show, Mrs. Nagle never complained, in fact, turned instead to humor. As she was going into the ring after having received no prizes in all the prior classes in which she had entered quality dogs, she turned to a friend and with that well-known mischievous twinkle in her eye said so that no one could hear, "Abandon all hope, ye who enter here."

In addition to these noteworthy incidents that indicate both the onset of a new and challenging era and the firm guidance of continuity in a turbulent age, the decade witnessed "new" and "young" faces, names, kennels, and hounds who have become familiar to the entire fancy in the 1980s. Mrs. Thomas Powers, Powerscourt Kennels, imported several major hounds that won important victories during the decade. Her homebred Ch. Powerscourt Shanahan Thomas won the 1977 IWCA Specialty. Mrs. Mary Major, now a judge as well as breeder, and her late husband Harold, made her Major Acres Kennels a force on the West Coast and around the country. Her imported Magnus of Arraglen won a West Coast Specialty, as did her Ch. Major Acres Branwyn, F.C. at the age of ten and a half.

Ch. Fleetwind Roonagh, owned by Mr. and Mrs. Norman Hall, was Best of Opposite Sex at the West Coast Specialty in 1963 and Best of Breed at the same event in 1964 and again in 1967. She is shown here winning under the celebrated breeder-judge Miss Mary Jane Ellis. *Joan Ludwig*

Ch. Hillaway's Padraic of Eagle, owned by Samuel Evans Ewing III, established a good record as a winner and a producer. His victories include Best of Opposite Sex at the 1965 IWCA Specialty, Best of Breed at the 1966 IWCA Specialty—scoring from the Veterans class—and was Hound of the Year for 1964 and 1965. He was also the sire of twenty-three champions. *William Gilbert*

Donna Elzer's Keystone Kennels became a force to be reckoned with not only on the West Coast but also at IWCA Specialties. In a rare occurrence, she brought her homebred Garda Siocana Keystone Doc all the way to Ludwig's Corners, Pennsylvania, by air, showed him to Best of Winners, and became the first possessor of the coveted Starbuck trophy for the Best Irish Wolfhound bred by the exhibitor.

Mrs. Norman (Lois) Hall, now Thomasson, faithfully and gracefully reported events on the West Coast to *Harp and Hound* during the decade. After a close association with Mrs. Starbuck in her later years, Mrs. Thomasson made Fleetwind Kennels perhaps the best-known kennel of Irish Wolfhounds on the West Coast. Fleetwind Chellis, who won two West Coast Specialties, and her large, typical Fleetwind Frona, were only two of her many hounds that achieved success in the show rings on the West Coast and around the country. Furthermore, her breeding stands behind the greatest Irish Wolfhound Specialty winner of all time—Mrs. Bregy's Ch. Wild Isle Warlock.

THE 1970s POPULATION EXPLOSION

In 1969, *Harp and Hound* reported with joy the record 111 hounds present at the Specialty that year. Those figures should have sounded an alarm. Despite some forebodings, however, contemporaries assumed that more hounds automatically meant more *typical* hounds, and that more Wolfhound people automatically translated into more *responsible* owners and *better* breeders. Such is the advantage hindsight bestows that, looking back, observers should have realized the danger. Beginning in the 1970s, the breed stalwarts and their families could no longer by themselves act as custodians of the breed. In 1970, that was difficult to perceive, and probably impossible to accept, particularly for those who cherished the rapidly diminishing ways of the immediate post–World War II era. After spending the late 1960s in England, where my wife and I acquired our first Irish Wolfhound, coming home in 1970 was akin to major culture shock.

The Irish Wolfhound world in England—as so many other things English—happily lagged behind the United States. The dog, owner, and breeder population explosion did not occur in England until later. They are only feeling its full effects now, when most of us in America have already accepted and responded to it. Many factors contributed to this lag, not the least of which were England's being a smaller country and the continued presence of experienced breeders who dominated the world of Irish Wolfhounds by controlling their breeding, exhibition, and ownership. It was a world where most Wolfhound people knew each other, where most owners went to all the major shows (as they still do), and where a uniformity of type prevailed to a much greater extent than in the United States. Long-established kennels—Sulhamstead, Brabyns, Sanctuary, Boroughbury, and Eaglescrag—dominated the English world of Irish Wolfhounds. Furthermore, their strains were represented at all the major shows throughout the year, unless the breeder was judging.

Novices found it difficult, even forbidding at times, to enter this formidable world dominated by the established kennels. Nevertheless, they respected and deferred to the vast experience that these established breeders possessed. All of us fortunate enough to have entered the world of Wolfhounds during those years in England now know what a vast advantage we had over all those who would follow. We truly did learn from the masters. We saw their dogs teeming with overall type, fixed by carefully linebreeding the oldest stock, beautifully presented in the show ring in the most natural, pleasing manner, and living in surroundings that seemed to bring out the best in the hounds. We didn't talk much; there was too much to learn by listening. We didn't do much; there was too much to learn by watching. But we asked questions. And the answers came patiently, caringly, and knowledgeably. Many were the hours that Mrs. Nagle, Mrs. Jenkins, and Miss Hudson, my major teachers, spent showing me their dogs, steeping me in the history of the breed, and advising me on how to go about acquiring, caring for, and owning Irish Wolfhounds.

How different it all seemed when we returned from living in England in 1970. I remember going to my first dog show here. All the dogs looked different—they could have been three or four breeds, a few like Mastiffs, many more very tall. (I remember what a shock it was to see so many tall dogs, the tallest I'd ever seen.) Without exception, they proved to me two points, one made by Mrs. Jenkins, the other by Mrs. Nagle. Mrs. Nagle taught me that bigger is not always better. A look at these enormous dogs, and many more since, proved how right she was. Mrs. Jenkins told me about a disappointing development in a hound she owned: "He grew taller and taller, and as he grew taller he got straight shoulders and straighter stifles."

This collection of huge, straight dogs proved how Mrs. Jenkins's observation about her one dog applied generally.

Of course, we in America had our experts too, and they were the equals of those in England. But due to the size of the country, so enormous compared to England, and the nature of the American population, so much less deferential to authority, the experts' experience got spread too thin, and that weaker authority was diminished still further by the temper of the times.

By the early 1970s, experienced observers recognized the problems that the explosive growth in numbers generated. They no longer welcomed numbers that were staggeringly large and whose negative consequences were all too obvious, particularly the dilution and dispersion of type. How could they ignore them any longer? From fewer than 100 registrations a year during the 1950s to more than 500 in 1970, and 1,251 in 1972! The fancy had grown from a few dozen families and their friends in 1960 to triple the number in a comparatively short time. Many were largely unknown, often naive, and too often, even if rarely, profit- and glory-seeking novices applying for membership in the IWCA. Beyond the numbers applying for membership, and the members owning, showing, and breeding, was a whole new world of commercial and other breeders wholly ignorant of breed type, physiology, and temperament. The situation was ominously reflected in the repeated and more dire reports of Irish Wolfhounds in pet shops and dog pounds, Irish Wolfhound "puppy mills," mistreatment, and worse.

One incident in the 1970s proved a point that Mrs. Jenkins once made: well-meaning people without knowledge can cause more damage to the breed than commercial breeders. A man had recently bred a litter of Irish Wolfhounds because he thought it would be fun and good for his kids. No malice, no thirst for profit or lust for glory—just pleasure and experience for his family, a story I am sure many reading this book have heard, or perhaps have even experienced firsthand. The man came to me trying to find homes for, as I recall, ten puppies! I asked the usual questions—too late of course: Did you think about where these puppies would live when you bred this bitch? Why do you want to sell them now? Well, no, he hadn't thought about where they would live, and he just didn't realize how difficult it would be to care for all those big puppies. I was really angry, telling him I knew of no one who wanted his puppies. There may always be a demand for well-bred, good Irish Wolfhounds, but it will be difficult to find good homes for the others.

Ch. Ballykelly Powerscourt Tomas, Best of Breed, 1971 IWCA Specialty. "Rangy red wheaten Irish import . . . also won unofficial gait class"—*Harp and Hound*. Owned by Dr. and Mrs. Thomas Powers.

Ch. Boroughshane of Eagle, Best of Breed, 1972 IWCA Specialty. Bred, owned, and handled by Samuel E. Ewing III.

He tried, and so did I, to find good homes for the puppies. I will say for him, he really wanted to find them *good homes,* not just *anyplace* for them to live. He couldn't find good homes, and he couldn't afford to feed them. Through my mind passed the horrible and unspeakable thought that I should buy these puppies from him, take them to my vet, and put them down if I couldn't find them decent homes. He and I parted ways. At the time, I didn't realize how preferable death would have been for those puppies compared to the conditions of neglect and abuse under which they would be forced to live. The horror stories that resulted from his and others' ignorance, the greed of some, and my lack of courage, illustrate the consequences almost sure to follow from the deadly combination of ignorance, greed, self-indulgence, and the lack of a sense of responsibility for our own actions.

A motorist killed one of those puppies on the road; no one knows if it had an owner. A hiker found another starving in the woods somewhere in western Wisconsin. An animal lover rescued another—starving, parasite- and disease-ridden—from a dark, damp garage near where we lived in Minneapolis. As I recall, one found a good home; the others—who knows what end befell them? Who cares to imagine it? I have learned since that experience the advantages of a quick, painless death to a life of suffering from lack of food, shelter, and equally important, responsible love. Life does not often offer us easy choices between good and bad. The 1970s did not differ, nor do the 1980s, nor will the 1990s—we were, and are, forced occasionally to choose between a humane death and a miserable life.

It was an unfortunate irony of the 1970s that just when the *need* for knowledge was greatest, *recognizing* the need for it and discovering the *means* to disseminate what knowledge existed diminished. The world of Irish Wolfhounds was divided into three parts (and still is): (1) experienced, responsible, devoted owners and breeders, steeped in the history of the breed, who knew and understood breed type and were prepared to share their expertise with all who sought to learn; (2) large numbers of people without knowledge either of Irish Wolfhounds or how to learn about them; and (3) a band of selfish, greedy individuals without knowledge about, or a sense of responsibility to, the Irish Wolfhound, but eager to exploit the ignorance, gullibility, and affluence of the times for their own ends.

The Irish Wolfhound of today is fortunate—as future generations will be—to have had during the 1970s a core of experienced and responsible breeders, not all of whom can be acknowledged in these

Ch. Kihone Mearose of Cu, Best of Breed, 1973 IWCA Specialty. "This bitch has everything you want and despite the heat moved beautifully and willingly"—Winnifred Heckman, Specialty judge.

Ch. Wild Isle Warlock (Ch. Wild Isle Wizard ex Ch. Mistimourne Wild Isle Mirage), Best of Breed and Best of Winners, at fourteen months, IWCA Specialty, 1974. Bred, owned, and exhibited by Mrs. J. R. Bregy.

pages. I relate a few words about one of them here—although they do full justice neither to him nor to the others—in order both to reassure and to encourage us all. I first met this breeder in the early 1970s during his effort to help an owner who had bought a puppy from him. One day he called me on the telephone. I had never met nor seen him; he lived nearly two thousand miles away. A young woman living a few miles from me who owned one of his dogs "sounded as if" she might be having problems. Would it inconvenience me to go over there and check out the situation? He was prepared to come, but it would take time to get there by air, and he would like to know "now" if there really was a problem. If I thought there was, could I bring the dog to my kennel, keep him there until we could make arrangements to return him to the breeder? Would I assure the woman that the breeder would either return the woman's money (she had owned the dog at least a few years), send her another puppy, or anything else that *she* found acceptable? I went to the home—a good one—found out the problem was not serious, called the breeder to reassure him, and all went on as before. Please notice several things about this episode: The breeder asked me to check out a *possible* problem; he did not wait for something serious to actually happen. Second, he did not ask me to go to the woman for his convenience, but because he thought the dog and his owner might be in trouble. Third, he was prepared not only to return the woman's money but to entertain any arrangement that she found acceptable in spite of the long interval following the sale. Most people know Sam Ewing as a master showman and possessor of great wins. His acts as a responsible breeder, performed without fanfare, such as this one, stand as examples for all of us.

Greedy, irresponsible business people eager to profit from the giant dog business made up the second group. These could range from well-heeled, slick operators to barnyard breeders who saw Irish Wolfhounds simply as livestock. We had a few of each in Minnesota during those years. One smooth operator trumpeted it about that he was going to make the Wolfhound accessible to all—take it from the hands of the elite eastern snobs and put it in the hands of the "people." He advertised the hundred-dollar Wolfhound. He survived for a while until, fortunately, he discovered the truth of a front-page *Wall Street Journal* article—that breeding giant dogs for profit was a financial disaster in all cases. Unfortunately, he didn't discover it until he duped many residents of Minnesota and surrounding states into believing they had acquired the "peoples' Irish Wolfhound."

Soon they didn't want these expensive status symbols, and the "people's Wolfhounds" found their way into the dog pounds' destruction units. I have learned that most people who adopt Irish Wolfhounds are like most people who adopt babies. The vast majority of Irish Wolfhound people do not want just *any* Irish Wolfhound to love— they want a *good* Irish Wolfhound to love!

At the other end of the commercial breeder spectrum was a pathetically ignorant pig farmer who thought he could raise Irish Wolfhounds like livestock. That was not the worst: he didn't even know how to raise pigs! His pigs and hounds lived in unspeakable filth, inadequate or no shelter, were riddled with parasites, and often had no food or the food they got was tainted, foul, and insufficient. One woman, still a lover of our breed who never sought and does not now seek recognition, visited him, tried to reason with him, then tried to cajole him, and eventually angrily threatened him to do better by his dogs. She bought a few from him—just to love them and to save them from him. He didn't want to hurt his "stock." He didn't know any better. Too many dogs, and some people, suffered from his ignorance.

The negative consequences of the population explosion were now clear to all who opened their eyes and ears. Type had seriously deteriorated. A series of judges responded to a question *Harp and Hound*'s editor posed in 1973: "Has the quality of entries in Irish Wolfhound breed competition benefited or suffered from the great rise in registrations?"

Mary Jane Ellis, who has lived with Irish Wolfhounds most of her life, has studied them, seen them, and judged them both here and abroad, noted:

> The quality in the present-day Irish Wolfhound has not kept up with the quantity being shown in the United States. It is only at the Irish Wolfhound Club of America Specialty show that one can breathe a sigh of relief because one does find enough quality there to realize that there is a very small nucleus of beautiful hounds in this country. On this small nucleus one rests one's hope for the breed. These are hounds with substance and all the curves where they should be, are in beautiful condition, have symmetry and above all possess type and good temperament.

Mrs. Potter Wear, longtime Whippet breeder and hound judge, noted that Irish Wolfhounds suffered not only from serious specific faults but also from the dangerous lack of overall type in general and the dispersion into two extremes in particular. On the one hand were coarse hounds, lacking the requisite capacity for speed to catch wolves. On the other, she noted those tall, straight hounds who obviously lacked the strength to bring down a wolf. Mrs. Wear's remarks clearly demonstrate that type was perilously close to disintegrating into the parts that Graham and all his followers for nearly a century had joined so carefully, tirelessly, and with such commitment. The ancient breed, restored by judicious blending with others less commanding, less swift, but stronger, might have been lost. The persistent, inherent tension between the Mastiff and the Greyhound type was brought into bold, clear relief in the 1970s.

General Alfred W. de Quoy, the erudite modern scholar of the breed, himself a breeder-judge, answered *Harp and Hound*'s query in the language of statistics, which he speaks so familiarly:

> Today Irish Wolfhounds approach the Standard of Excellence in greater numbers than they did ten years ago. . . . Let us not, however, jump to the wrong conclusion. . . . There are more quality dogs because there are more "reputable" breeders. There is a larger percentage of poor dogs because the number of ill-advised or ignorant breeders and the number of puppy mills has greatly increased. So that, while there are more quality Irish Wolfhounds and while these have shown great improvement, especially in the hindquarters, the percentage is less than it was ten years ago.

The story of Irish Wolfhounds in the 1970s was not all dark. The Irish Wolfhound Club of America, its publication *Harp and Hound,* the established regional clubs—the Irish Wolfhound Association of the West Coast and the Irish Wolfhound Association of New England—and individual owners everywhere responded creatively, if not always totally successfully, to the consequences of overpopulation. The IWCA expanded its board of directors to include more regional representation, reluctantly accepting the reality of the new, bigger world of Irish Wolfhounds. The Northeast, the Mid-Atlantic states, and California no longer contained most of the Irish Wolfhounds. Members from the Eastern Seaboard, however, dominated the IWCA.

California had had a long association with the parent club; the breed and IWCA's longest-standing stalwarts, Mrs. Smith and Mrs. Starbuck, had migrated to California, operated extremely successful kennels there, and remained there for the rest of their lives. From the 1960s, Mrs. Lois Hall, Fleetwind Kennels, had reported California

Ch. Wild Isle Warlock (Ch. Wild Isle Wizard ex Ch. Mistimourne Wild Isle Mirage), Best of Breed, IWCA Specialty, 1975. Bred, owned, and exhibited by Mrs. J. R. Bregy.

Ch. Wild Isle Warlock (Ch. Wild Isle Wizard ex Ch. Mistimourne Wild Isle Mirage), Best of Breed, IWCA Specialty, 1976. Bred, owned, and exhibited by Mrs. J. R. Bregy.

Wolfhound news in *Harp and Hound.* The expanded board of directors included more regional representation. By the late 1970s, all major areas in the country had at least a formal voice in the IWCA. The IWCA reached out in other significant ways. The Club, barring 1951 (Long Beach, California) and 1968 (Wichita, Kansas), had always held its "National" Specialty along the East Coast, never farther south than Virginia. During the 1970s, the Club met twice in Wisconsin, and twice in Ohio, for its Specialties and annual meetings. Board meetings moved around as well, being held sometimes in the Midwest, sometimes in the East, and once or twice on the West Coast. The Club also established a list of responsible breeders and owners in all states so that interested persons inquiring about Irish Wolfhounds could learn about the hounds from principled, knowledgeable people. Probably no single individual did more during this period than Jane Moir, secretary and later president of the IWCA, both to answer inquiries from throughout the country and to match interested persons with responsible owners and breeders in the same locality. The Club continues this valuable operation as a regular part of its responsibilities to the breed, as well as to those who want to own Irish Wolfhounds.

Harp and Hound, the IWCA's educational arm, also responded positively to the population explosion. Its devoted editor, Rosalie Fox, Cu Kennels, recognized and responded to regional differences by introducing a new feature in the publication, the regional reports, a practice the present editor, Mrs. Gretchen Bernardi, has happily continued, with some modifications. Reporting from all parts of the country provided a communications network that drew the far-flung world of Irish Wolfhounds closer together throughout the year, and for those who could not attend Specialties, it provided the best official link to the hounds, owners, and breeders. *Harp and Hound* also became much more educational under Mrs. Fox's editorship. More columns appeared that dealt with problems of ownership, what to do about puppy mills, and rescue operations. In addition to these new problems, columns about feeding, rearing, showing, breeding, buying, and selling Irish Wolfhounds appeared. Principled novices hungered for such information and responded with demands for even more "help."

Harp and Hound could not meet all the educational needs, let alone the demands, that inexperienced owners, and increasingly breeders, brought about. Countless individuals around the country tended to Wolfhound "affairs" in their local communities. These

Ch. Wild Isle Warlock (Ch. Wild Isle Wizard ex Ch. Mistimourne Wild Isle Mirage), Best of Breed, IWCA Specialties, 1974, 1975, 1976, and 1979—the all-time record IWCA Specialty winner, shown here winning Best of Breed from the Veterans class. Bred, owned, and handled by Mrs. J. R. Bregy.

Ch. Powerscourt Shanahan, Best of Breed, 1977 IWCA Specialty, "demonstrated himself to be a living version of the Standard—a typical, sound hound"—Roxanne Bleeker, Specialty judge. Bred and owned by Dr. and Mrs. Thomas Powers.

people, known and unknown, devoted to the Irish Wolfhound and working without trumpeting it about, blunted the consequences of too many inexperienced people buying from too many commercial and other ignorant breeders. Some combed their areas looking for commercialism and ignorance, and tried to combat it by educating individuals themselves. Others watched their local newspapers for Wolfhound ads, responding to them in order to learn who was selling, why, and in what conditions they raised their puppies and kept their "breeding stock." Some placed ads in the pet sections of local newspapers, some bought space in local all-breed-show catalogues throughout those troubled years. One ad that appeared regularly in newspapers and dog-show catalogues read: "Caution: Before you buy an Irish Wolfhound puppy from a newspaper ad, call [a local breeder's number]."

These informal efforts to reach those without education by advertisement uncovered a vast number of principled people who wanted to do the right thing but did not know how. We invited them to see our dogs at home, see if they *really* wanted such a big dog. I can remember keeping unfilled the enormous holes dug by puppies in what used to be a beautiful lawn, leaving standing a once fruit-laden apple tree now dead because a hound had stripped the bark from its trunk, and keeping a "topless" picnic table with the planks two very active puppies had ripped from its base. I showed these to every interested person. Then I let the dogs out onto the lawn so that the visitors could see what it means to have an Irish Wolfhound next to them. This always separates interested people into two groups, happily *before* they buy an Irish Wolfhound. It is a curious thing, but I have found that individuals do not respond halfheartedly to Irish Wolfhounds. Close contact with several adult hounds immediately demonstrates this. Every person I have ever had visit here, after seeing the holes, the apple tree, the picnic table, and having several adult hounds right up next to them, decides one of two things right there and then: Irish Wolfhounds are *not* for me; or, I have *got* to have an Irish Wolfhound. Only one person out of all who bought dogs from me decided later that he did not want Irish Wolfhounds. The rest will love the breed for life.

With Irish Wolfhounds at least, people either love them forever or want little or nothing to do with them. A recent visitor to my kennel represents the typical Wolfhound person. He saw me reading old *Harp and Hound*s in a Minneapolis café. He approached me to tell me that he had always admired the Irish Wolfhound, and everything he read made him want to know about them firsthand. I invited him to the kennel. He came a few days later, scrubbed clean, with a crisp, newly pressed light blue shirt and spotlessly *white* trousers. I mentioned that it was too bad he was so clean because the recent heavy rains had left mudholes where the dogs lived. The dogs, if let out, would get him dirty. He was petting them over the fence, and said, "Please let them out, I can wash my clothes." I did, and he loved every minute of the contact with them. A student at the University of Minnesota, he was leaving Minneapolis for the summer, but he asked if he could pay another visit as soon as summer break ended. That is a *true* Wolfhound person. We should know that *before* they buy a dog. Many people around the country work to find this out by introducing all who are interested to Irish Wolfhounds *before* they buy them. Then they introduce those who *know* they want an Irish Wolfhound to respectable breeders.

The growing numbers of hounds and people in regions throughout the country prompted not only regional representation on the IWCA board of directors, regional reports in *Harp and Hound*, and informal individual responses in local communities. The 1970s, and even more so the 1980s, saw the proliferation of regional "clubs" that ranged across a broad organizational spectrum. In addition to the two oldest regional clubs, the Irish Wolfhound Association of the West Coast and the Irish Wolfhound Association of New England, new clubs sprung up around the country. They included: the Irish Wolfhound Association of Delaware Valley, the Irish Wolfhound Club of Potomac Valley, the Irish Wolfhound Club of Greater New Jersey, the Irish Wolfhound Club of Central New York, the Irish Wolfhound Club of the South, the Irish Wolfhound Club of Greater Chicago, the Heartland Irish Wolfhound Club, the Locust Grove Irish Wolfhound Club, the Rocky Mountain Irish Wolfhound Association, the Midwest Irish Wolfhound Association, the Irish Wolfhound Club of Puget Sound, the Irish Wolfhound Club of Northern California, and Friends of the Irish Wolfhound (Ohio).

Some, such as the Irish Wolfhound Association of the West Coast and the Irish Wolfhound Association of Delaware Valley, hold their own Specialties. Others, such as the Locust Grove Irish Wolfhound Club, exist mainly to have an annual fun match, one of the pleasantest events of the year. Judges come from abroad and from all over the country to judge the hounds—no points, just the judge's opinion. Mrs. Stannye Musson, Louisville, Kentucky, whose Maghera Glass Kennels has owned several top-winning Irish Wolfhounds, originated the Locust Grove Fun Match. Dr. and Mrs. Robert Bernardi, Berwyck Kennels, have continued the event. The event, held first at Mrs. Musson's residence, and now at the Bernardis', is a wonderful, social, all-day event. Not simply the judging, but the lunch and dinner at the Bernardis', offers the opportunity to see and "talk" dogs, learn, and be in the company of others with similar interests.

Newer clubs have emulated the older organizations, some sponsoring matches as a step to eventually holding Specialties, others desiring no more than to bring interested people together for a day of learning, fun, and friendly competition. The Irish Wolfhound Association of the West Coast holds an annual fun match, aimed mainly at education and fun. Workshops on grooming, showing, and handling Irish Wolfhounds make up half the day; a fun match rounds it out. Mrs. Pat Huntley's passionate commitment to the breed she loves, and her unswerving belief that education holds the best promise for maintaining the Irish Wolfhound, are the inspirations for the event. Mrs. Huntley told me once that her grandmother used to say: "You know, Pat, you can send a stick around the world and it will come back still a stick." Mrs. Huntley obviously believes that few people interested in Irish Wolfhounds fall into the "stick" category. Without the population increase, the regional clubs, and their valuable and varied functions, probably would not exist today. The world of Wolfhounds would be the poorer without them.

By the early 1980s, these clubs and their activities were well-established parts of the world of Irish Wolfhounds. Clubs either did or did not seek American Kennel Club recognition, depending on the group's needs, interests, and desires. Former IWCA president Eugenia Hunter, Ironwood Kennels, writing about the Locust Grove Irish Wolfhound Club's decision not to seek AKC recognition, pointed to several advantages:

> Without AKC recognition, a local club may do any of the things it could do as a recognized club except give a point-show. The club may have matches, educational events, do rescue, and have meetings. But also the club may offer special classes [for example, neutered dog and spayed bitch], classes for 3-month to 6-month puppies, and new three-win trophies, have more variety in selection of judges, and hold the matches outside a local area on grounds which the AKC might not approve.
>
> Locust Grove has done all of these "non-regular" things and by all accounts has prospered because of them.

Perhaps no other single event of the 1970s more glamorously portrayed the efforts to reach out and educate the expanding numbers of people interested in Irish Wolfhounds than the "Killybracken Get-Together" held at Killybracken Kennels in 1971 in Francestown, New Hampshire. Inspired and beautifully managed by the late Mrs. C. Groverman Ellis and Miss Mary Jane Ellis, for two days more than 160 people from all over the United States and Canada gathered to learn about Irish Wolfhounds from the experts. On the first day, the late Mrs. Nagle, Sulhamstead Kennels, England; Samuel Evans Ewing III, Eagle Kennels, Glen Mills, Pennsylvania; and the late Celeste Hutton, Greysarge Kennels, Maryland, judged twenty-two hounds, and then told the guests why they picked the hounds in the order they did. Except for a few minor placements, all the judges agreed. Those who listened to these experts learned valuable lessons about type, movement, soundness, and conformation. Watching three experts place hounds and then have them explain to the spectators *how* they judged taught everyone the intricacies of judging Irish Wolfhounds. Those attending also saw films comparing hounds from Ambleside in the 1920s with modern hounds, clips of Irish Wolfhounds in dog shows, and Mrs. Rachel Page Elliot's now well-known films on dog movement. There were panel discussions and demonstrations about rearing, feeding, grooming, showing, and breeding Irish Wolfhounds.

The Killybracken Get-Together was a historic event in and of itself. But in addition it inspired other, less-publicized duplicate events. Mrs. Nagle sponsored such a gathering at Westerlands, England, then home of Sulhamstead Kennels. She brought out her hounds one by one, and all who gathered "got their hands" on the dogs. We had to tell her what we were feeling for, what it felt like, and whether what we were feeling was correct. Then Mrs. Nagle explained to us how to "go over" a dog, what to look for, and why. All of us who attended learned three valuable lessons. First, we really learned what to feel for when we put our hands on the dogs. Second, we found out that what meets the eye does not reveal what only the hands can discover. That is why *knowledgeable* judges surprise *inexperienced* spectators by some of their choices in the show ring. Finally, we learned to forever withhold judgment on *sight* alone; *feeling* constitutes an indispensable element in assessing dogs.

Less spectacular than either the Killybracken or Sulhamstead Get-Togethers, but perhaps equally important in the long run, are groups that sponsored similar events around the United States.

Many small clusters of interested people and more or less experienced serious owners and breeders met to "go over" hounds, look at films, discuss the Irish Wolfhound Standard, and were inspired both to learn more themselves and to do more to educate others concerning the correct Irish Wolfhound type, care, feeding, rearing, and handling. The effects of these events still reverberate in the educational dimensions of many fun matches. All the regional clubs, and the informal gatherings not officially known, consider education central to their mission.

Trends, numbers, averages—these of course should not be overlooked in assessing Irish Wolfhounds during the 1970s. The 1970s were years when more academically oriented owners, and the "high-tech" world they inhabited, led to the belief that they could apply to breeding, selecting, and rearing Irish Wolfhounds the rules of pure science. The slide rule, not the artist's palate, seemed the more appropriate metaphor to describe this approach. At the Killybracken Get-Together, Mrs. Nagle criticized this new approach in memorable words:

> Let us all remember what we owe to the top breeders past and present and realize breeding is an art, not a science, and we can't just feed facts into a computer and come out with the perfect answer.

She elaborated on the point in her remarks at the judge's dinner following the 1974 IWCA Specialty:

> To be a good breeder is partly a gift, but it is like painting a picture with living animals, which is a very interesting occupation.

THE IRISH WOLFHOUND IN THE 1980s AND BEYOND

Computers and the rapid advance on all scientific and technological fronts surely cannot replace knowledge or supply the talent to breed, or to recognize, proper type in Irish Wolfhounds. However, it can provide valuable tools to those who wish to learn and who have the requisite ability for breeding good Irish Wolfhounds. The video camera and the proliferation of VCRs is a boon both for recording and for disseminating knowledge about our breed. Breeders send video recordings of their stock to other breeders and to interested persons who live too far away to see the dogs personally. Breeders

Meadowbrook Sir Lancelot (Ch. Garda Siocana Keystone Kilty ex Ch. Keystone Kilkerry), Best of Breed, 1978 IWCA Specialty, his first show, at seventeen months of age. "A balanced, typical, hound who felt just right when I went over him"—Judge Miss Noreen Twyman, Nendrum Kennels, Ireland. Bred and owned by Joel and Jennifer Samaha, handled by Joel Samaha.

Ch. Redtops Eirena (Ch. Wild Isle Warlock ex Ch. Elmbrae's Elegance of Redtop), Best of Breed IWCA Specialties, 1980, 1982, a beautifully made cream bitch, hard body, one of the best- "feeling" dogs I have ever gone over." Bred and owned by David and Rosemary Wortman, and handled by Rosemary Wortman.

record their stock from birth to adulthood, providing a record for the future.

Since 1985, the Irish Wolfhound Club of America has recorded each IWCA Specialty; several regional clubs have followed suit. These recordings are already a valuable archive of the late-twentieth-century Irish Wolfhound. The IWCA does not intend for these recordings to remain archived; anyone interested can purchase copies of them from the IWCA. The advances in artificial insemination and the American Kennel Club's recent sanctioning of the procedure have vastly enhanced the potential for long-distance matings. Still in its infancy vis-à-vis dogs, but rapidly catching on, artificial insemination will at least reduce, and perhaps in the future virtually eliminate, the need to ship dogs long distances to breed them.

These, and other new developments in science and technology, used properly by those who have the ability and good sense to benefit from them, can become forces for great good for the Irish Wolfhound. They may also, of course, enhance the potential for harm. Bad, as well as good, breedings can result from shipping semen long distances; science and technology can execute all artificial insemination. Possessing video recordings can never substitute for understanding and appreciating the recordings' contents. Neither artificial insemination nor recordings can ever act as satisfactory substitutes for natural breeding and actual observation. Nor can statistical analyses ever stand proxy for the art of breeding.

One dog during the 1970s dominated the statistics *and* caught the eye of some of the breed's most respected judges—Ch. Wild Isle Warlock, bred, owned, and always handled by Mrs. Jill Richards Bregy, Wild Isle Kennels. No Irish Wolfhound won more IWCA Specialties—Warlock holds the record with four. He won his first at fourteen months under the English breeder-judge Mrs. Nagle in 1974; from the Veterans class, the Canadian all-rounder Mrs. Norden awarded him his last in 1979. Two other breeder-judges, Mrs. Rosalie Fox, Cu Kennels, and Mrs. Ruth Jenkins, Eaglescrag Kennels, Wales, awarded Warlock IWCA Specialty wins over record entries. In addition to the IWCA Specialty, Warlock won the Canadian Specialty (IWCC) three times, and the New England Specialty (IWANE) four times. Warlock was undefeated in the Specialties he entered. In his first show, he went from the Puppy class to Best of Breed and a five-point major; at fourteen months, in his second show, the 1974 IWCA Specialty, he won Best in Show; and in his third show, where he finished his championship, he went from the Bred-by-Exhibitor class to Best in Show at an all-breed event—at seventeen months!

Perhaps even more dramatic, Warlock sired a two-time IWCA Specialty winner, Redtops Eirena, owned by Mrs. Rosemary Wortman, Redtops Kennels. The 1983 IWCA Specialty displayed Warlock's get's most impressive Specialty victories. Virginia Hardin, former handler for Ambleside, Killybracken, and other leading Irish Wolfhound Kennels, judged. She awarded Ch. Redtops Eirena Best of Breed (Ch. Wild Isle Warlock ex Ch. Elbrae's Elegance of Redtop), Ch. Fitzarran Dudly of Whitehall (Ch. Wild Isle Warlock ex Ch. Eaglescrag Kate) Best of Opposite Sex, Wildisle Alpha Sirius (Ch. Wild Isle Warlock ex Ch. Lilliput My Lady Lenore) Best of Winners, and Hope of Whitehall (Ch. Wild Isle Warlock ex Ch. Honey Voo Greta Garbo) Reserve Winners Bitch.

Warlock serviced approximately thirty bitches, from whom many dogs in the 1990s descend. In fact, few dogs entered in Irish Wolfhound Specialties do not descend from Warlock on at least one, if not both, sides of their pedigree. Warlock was the paternal great-grandsire to Mr. and Mrs. Robert Gilb's Ch. Sharbo Gunther (Ch. Pioneer Stutz Bearcat ex Ch. Magherglas Dulcimer), Best of Breed 1986 IWCA Specialty; the maternal grandsire to Phillippa Crowe Nielson's Kingsland Song (Ch. Fitzarran Shadowfax ex Ch. Fitzarran Kingsland Koren), Best of Breed 1987 IWCA Specialty; the paternal great-grandsire to Mr. and Mrs. William Peacy's Ch. Marcmora Fame's Odyssey (Ch. Weylin Willie of Whitehall ex Ch. Fame of Marcmora); and the paternal great-grandsire to Dr. and Mrs. Robert Bernardi's Witchesbroom Berwyck Uther (Ch. Berwyck Navarre ex Witchesbroom Mapleton Sorceress), Best of Breed 1989 IWCA Specialty.

Mrs. Rosemary Wortman's Redtops Eirena became the 1980s top Specialty winner. She won two IWCA Specialties—1980 under all-rounder and long-time Irish Wolfhound lover Tom Stevenson, and 1982 under Virginia Hardin. Only her famous sire's unique four Specialty wins surpass Eirena's spectacular victories. In addition to two IWCA Specialty wins, Eirena won each of the following *twice!*— the New England Specialty (IWANE), the Canadian Specialty (IWCC), the Ontario Sighthound show. She also won four Bests in Show at all-breed events. In 1984, Warlock's get continued to score impressive wins at the IWCA Specialty. At the time to choose Best of Breed, Mrs. Rosalie Fox, Cu Kennels, had eliminated all but fourteen hounds—eleven descended from Warlock! Warlock sired the Best of Opposite Sex, Ch. Hope of Whitehall, owned by Mr. and Mrs. Frank Dean, Whitehall Kennels, and was the grandsire to the Deans' Wild Valley Bravo Whitehall (Ch. Fitzarran Dudly of White-hall ex Zarahemla Wild Valley Song).

Mrs. Fox awarded the top win, Best of Breed, to Mr. Samuel Evans Ewing III's Ch. Aodh Harp of Eagle (Ch. Karn's Malin of Eagle ex Ch. Cugael Arrabeth Harp of Eagle), thus ending Warlock and Eirena's nearly decade-long domination of the top wins at IWCA, New England, and Canadian Specialties. Between 1974 and 1983, only three in addition to Warlock and Eirena won Best of Breed at IWCA Specialties: 1977—Dr. and Mrs. Powers' Ch. Powers-court Shannahan (Ch. High and Mighty of Carrickmines ex Ch. Cromlech of Eaglescrag); 1978—Joel and Jennifer Samaha's Mead-owbrook Sir Lancelot (Ch. Garda Siocana Keystone Kilty ex Ch. Keystone Kilkerry); and 1983—Mr. and Mrs. William Pfarrer's, Piuritan Kennels, and Mr. Samuel Evans Ewing III's Piuritan Pris-cilla (Ch. More of Eagle ex Ch. Piuritan Muslin of Eagle). Ch. Aodh Harp of Eagle's fame spread beyond Best of Breed at the 1984 IWCA Specialty. "Hughie" won fifteen all-breed Bests in Show, topping the record held by his great-grandsire, Mr. Ewing's Ch. Boroughshane of Eagle (Windale Ridire Dubh of Eagle ex Boroughbury Brona), IWCA Best of Breed in 1972.

Mr. Ewing's famed Eagle Kennels' breeding lay behind both the 1983 and 1985 Specialty Bests of Breed as well. Mrs. Zena Andrews, Drakesleat Kennels, England, awarded Mr. and Mrs. W. Sullivan Pfarrer's and Samuel Evans Ewing III's Piuritan Priscilla Best of Breed in 1983; and Mr. Joel Samaha, Meadowbrook Kennels, awarded Mrs. Anne Tweer's Ch. Brandy Whines Morah of Eagle Best of Breed in 1985; both were sired by Ch. More of Eagle, grand-son of Ch. Boroughshane of Eagle.

Captain Graham saved the ancient giant Greyhound-like Wolf-dog from oblivion in the nineteenth century. The stewards of the first half of the twentieth century ably preserved Captain Graham's work, and the stewards who steered the breed through the stormy 1960s and 1970s deserve credit for preventing the disintegration of type beyond recovery. As we entered the last decade of the twentieth century, all who loved the Irish Wolfhound in its ancient character could breathe more easily. All around us the signs were good. Breed-ers, and breeder- and all-round judges, both from here and abroad, noticed marked improvement in quality, soundness, and type at the end of the 1980s over what it had been just ten years before.

Ch. Magmellan Fitzwilliam Avoca (Avoca Ice Man ex Mona Macushla of Elmbrae), Best of Breed, Best of Winners, IWCA Specialty, 1981. "A rare dog... beautifully balanced... quality and type"—Judge, Miss Mary Jane Ellis, Killybracken Kennels, and formerly Sulhamstead Kennels. Owned by Mrs. William R. Morrison, bred by Mrs. A. J. de Villiers.

Ch. Piuritan Priscilla (Ch. More of Eagle ex Ch. Piuritan Muslin of Eagle), Best of Breed and Best of Winners, IWCA Specialty, 1983. "A most feminine bitch with quality right through.... Conformation right through of the very best"—Zena Andrews, Drakesleat Kennels, England. Bred by Mr. and Mrs. William A. Pfarrer, owned by Mr. and Mrs. Pfarrer and Mr. Samuel E. Ewing III.

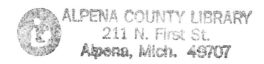
75

Mrs. Kelly (Rosalie) Fox, Cu Kennels, long-time breeder, owner, and twice the IWCA Specialty judge, made these encouraging remarks following the judging of a record entry of more than three hundred dogs at the IWCA 1984 Specialty:

> I have never seen so much quality at any Specialty—in such depth, particularly the two classes where nearly every entry was a star: Novice Bitches and 12–18 Month Bitches. . . .
>
> Enormous as the ring was, the 64 Irish Wolfhounds [in competition for Best of Breed] entered, and soon there was room only for them to walk in close order. Having slowly circled the ring and been given the signal to stand, those silent and majestic creatures made a magnificent picture—an historic picture—which surely must live long in one's mind's eye and memory.

About the Best of Breed, Ch. Aodh Harp of Eagle, Mrs. Fox commented:

> One is instantly struck by the ideal proportion, size and outline of this Wolfhound who personifies the ideal male type—size without coarseness, substance without coarseness, a masculine head without coarseness. An ugly rumor has it that wheaten coats are by nature of poor quality. False! The three top-placed hounds—Best of Winners, Best Opposite, and Best of Breed, were all wheaten and each sported a superior coat surpassed by none, the latter with the most enhancing face furnishings.
>
> He moved out sound and true, his back in profile, a quiet line free of jounce not only because his leg action was in sync but because his superior front assembly precluded any pounding. His head! Balance and beauty. If my face conveyed to him the interest and friendliness I felt, he certainly returned it in kind with his direct and intelligent eye. Dark eyes, dark pigmentation; model feet. This grand Irish Wolfhound has in abundance what is presently a rare trait in our breed and yet is an integral part of Irish Wolfhound type: *a commanding bearing.*

I judged both the IWCA Specialty and the Irish Wolfhound Association of the West Coast Specialty in 1985. At both events, I was able to find depth of quality and soundness in every class. What particularly pleased me, and should reassure us all, is that in all top placements I could select dogs that filled my requirement of the tall, galloping, powerful Greyhound-like dog that Captain Graham and all his followers since saved from oblivion. Mrs. Anne Tweer's Ch. Brandy Whines Morah of Eagle, a balanced, powerful bitch best captured my mind's eye view of correct type. All the finalists in that

Ch. Aodh Harp of Eagle (Ch. Karn's Malin of Eagle ex Ch. Cugael Arabeth Harp of Eagle), Best of Breed, IWCA Specialty, 1984. Bred, owned, and handled by S. E. Ewing III.

Ch. More of Eagle (Petasmeade Barney ex Ch. Mistimourne Mullach of Eagle), sire of two IWCA Specialty Best of Breeds. Bred and owned by Samuel E. Ewing III.

last cut, however, were worthy contenders that reflected the great improvement in consistency of type that had taken place by the mid-1980s.

Just two months later, in July 1985, two thousand miles away in California, I was equally thrilled to see the dramatic improvement in quality, soundness, and type that I found in the entry presented to me. A year spent in California immediately following our return from living in England gave me the opportunity to follow the California hounds. I had even judged in California a few times during the late 1970s. But I was unprepared for the *extent* of the improvement. I felt compelled to turn to the ringside and point out to the spectators that the nine hounds remaining in the ring at the final cut were all worthy contenders—rough-coated, Greyhound-like dogs, swift enough to catch a wolf, and powerful enough to dispatch it. But it was my day to pick one of those hounds, and what a pleasure to find a ten-year-old Veteran Bitch, Richard and Yvonne Heskett's Ch. Major Acres Branwyn, F.Ch. (Ch. Major Acres Vanguard ex Ch. Major Acres Fannee Manahan), bred by Harold and Mary Major, as my favorite that day. Tall, deep, powerful, and moving effortlessly (at 90-plus degrees and at age ten!), she filled my eye, representing the powerful galloping dog in a Greyhound-like form. It was unfortunate—as it was two months earlier—that I could not award all those in the final cut something. Spectators and, sadly, often exhibitors do not realize that that final *group* of quality hounds in a Specialty represents the approximation of the judge's ideal type. But you have to pick one. I am pleased to have picked Morah and Branwyn; it was a personal satisfaction. But the other hounds, as a group, forcefully represented the generally strengthened type in the 1980s that bodes well for our breed's future.

Others confirmed my opinion that type, quality, and soundness had all improved by the mid-1980s. Mrs. Dot Arn, Arntara Kennels, then president of the Irish Wolfhound Club of America, noted in her president's message to the membership in 1986:

> It is encouraging to note the improvement in movement as witnessed at the last several Specialty shows. Breeders are to be commended for their efforts as well as those who have made the important contribution of teaching others about this essential aspect of our hounds. This year there was an abundance of hounds of fine quality from various parts of the country—a very uplifting sight to witness. What a joy to watch the Puppy classes, so filled with inexperience and promise.

Ch. Brandy Whines Morah of Eagle (Ch. More of Eagle ex Ch. Brandy Whines Tara Karn), Best of Breed, IWCA Specialty 1985. A bitch of type, symmetry, and balance to which I was proud to award top honors when I judged the 1985 Specialty. Bred, owned, and handled by Anne C. Tweer.

Ch. Sharbo Gunther (Ch. Pioneer Stutz Bearcat ex Ch. Magheraglas Dulcimer), Best of Breed, IWCA Specialty, 1986. Bred by R. and S. Gilb and J. Mackimm, and owned by R. and S. Gilb.

Mrs. Bregy, Wild Isle Kennels, after judging the 1986 Puget Sound Specialty, wrote in her critique:

> In several classes, including Specials, there was great depth of quality and I was able to choose winners as close to the ideal as possible and make few compromises in doing so. . . .
>
> Some outstanding dogs competing for Best of Breed. Lots of depth and quality to choose from which makes this a very nice win for Best of Breed Bitch Ch. Castlemaine Josephine [(Ch. Castlemaine Wee Willie ex Ch. Castlemaine Hillary of D), bred by Marilyn Shaw, owned by Marilyn and Greg Shaw]. A very beautiful hound. Moves with great strength, reach and drive. Never falters, undoubtedly due to her beautiful structure. Wonderful body type. An outstanding hound. She was pushed hard by Ch. Lilliput Xtraordinary Lass, a beautifully made bitch with a little more leg under her . . . movement.

Mrs. L. S. Jenkins, Eaglescrag Kennels, Wales, who had judged the IWCA Specialty in 1976, commented after judging more than three hundred hounds at the IWCA Specialty in 1987:

> I was asked by many how the breed as represented today compared with that which I judged eleven years ago. It was nice to be able to say that, in my humble opinion, significant progress has been made. More of today's exhibitors seemed to demonstrate a better appreciation of the Standard, as 1987 presented a lot more hound-like specimen, more shapely and with better movement. Being amongst so many good-quality hounds meant, of course, that many worthy exhibits were unplaced. I trust that the taking part in such a great Wolfhound occasion was itself a satisfaction. . . .
>
> I never cease to marvel at the Champion class. I thought about it and wondered what I could liken it to and I thought it was rather like standing in the middle of a huge bowl of cream. There you were, surrounded by all of this excellence. But, in the end, I was extremely satisfied with my Best in Show winner, Kingsland Song [(Ch. Fitzarran Shadowfax ex Ch. Fitzarran Kingsland Koren), bred and handled by Phillippa Crowe Nielson]. I think that, on the day, she stood out for all the things I was looking for—the lovely-quality head with the rather sad, far-looking eyes; the lovely, strong legs running into the well-made shoulder, firm topline with an arch over the loin and nice slope to croup; deep chest and just wide enough, not too broad. . . . There she was with nicely proportioned chest, good legs, sound feet, a nice tuck-up, good curve of stifle, nice breadth across the stifle, muscular thighs and second thighs, nice long tail well-carried. And she moved like a queen, so it was indeed her day.

Ch. Kingsland Song (Ch. Fitzarran Shadowfax ex Ch. Fitzarran Kingsland Koren), Best of Breed and Best of Winners, IWCA Specialty, 1987. "The more I studied her, the more she stood out for quality, balance, and substance"—Mrs. L. S. Jenkins, Specialty judge Eaglescrag Kennels, Wales. Bred, owned, and handled by Phillippa Crowe Nielson.   *Moments by Jane*

Ch. Marcmora Fame's Odyessy (Ch. Weylin Willie of Whitehall ex Ch. Fame of Marcmora), Best of Breed, IWCA Specialty, 1988. "He was just what I would want were I to search the world over for an Irish Wolfhound to show and breed from"—Mrs. Potter Wear, Whippet breeder, Specialty judge. Bred and owned by W. J. and S. L. Peacy.

Mr. Frank Sabella, multiple Group judge, commented following his judging the 1988 Irish Wolfhound Association of New England (IWANE) Specialty:

> Judging this specialty was an event I looked forward to with great anticipation. This was partially due to my concern about the quality of the animals that would be shown under me, and also judging a specialty is always a great way to define completely what one's interpretation of the Standard of the particular breed being passed upon is all about. . . .
>
> The part of the Standard that seemed to be most important for me was listed as number one in the list of points in order of merit and to quote: "The Irish Wolfhound is a rough-coated Greyhoundlike breed" and for me personally, I would have to add that it would be practically impossible for a Wolfhound to be typical without displaying a very positive degree of soundness when moving.
>
> For all present, the quality of animals spoke for itself and for those not there, I will say I was thrilled with the quality brought before me. [All the top winners demonstrated] the outline I was looking for. Winners Dog, Best of Winners, and Best of Breed, Fitzarran Comus [(Fitzarran Kinsman ex Fitzarran Mandan), bred and owned by William and Betty Deemer] typifies the breed for me both moving and standing. A wheaten dog blessed with wonderful head, eye and expression, great in outline with all parts of his body fitting together with great balance, I could watch this dog go around the ring all day. His clean, effortless movement was a joy to behold.

Judges and observers also noted that the Irish Wolfhound had far from reached perfection, and that breeders must remain ever vigilant lest we forfeit forever the fragile type of the reconstructed hound that Captain Graham so brilliantly wrought, that his successors so steadfastly conserved, and that we foolishly came perilously close to losing in the 1960s and 1970s. Mrs. Potter Wear, after she went over the hounds at the 1988 IWCA Specialty, although generally optimistic, noted the variety of type, particularly the tendency to fall into the two extremes—Saint Bernard and Deerhound:

> It was a thrill for me to judge the high-quality entry of Irish Wolfhounds that was presented to me for my appraisal at the annual specialty show. . . .
>
> There was the diversity of type that is to be expected in a large entry of any breed, and the differences ran the gamut from Deerhound (too fine) to Saint Bernard (too heavy). However, a healthy number fell

Witchesbroom Berwyck Uther (Ch. Berwyck Navarre ex Mapleton Sorceress), Best of Breed, IWCA Specialty, 1989, at seventeen months and his first time shown. "A stallion hound, well grown, balanced, and very typical with a firm, good temperament, a very pleasing hound to go over"—Mr. William Marriott, Mapleton Kennels, England. Owned by Dr. and Mrs. Robert Bernardi.

Ch. Karn's Fion Mac Rua of Eagle (Ch. An Dara's Mac of Eagle ex Ch. Karn's Faun of Eagle), Best of Breed at the Irish Wolfhound Club of America's 1990 Specialty under judge Sheila Kemp. In her critique, Mrs. Kemp observed ". . . he obviously felt 'Top Banana' and showed it." Bred and owned by Jacqueline Karpinski and Samuel Evans Ewing III.   *Alverson*

between these extremes into what is to me, correct type, which is to quote your Standard, "a rough-coated Greyhoundlike breed," the largest and tallest of the galloping hounds.

Furthermore, in Mrs. Wear's judgment, her choice for Best of Breed, Ch. Marcmora Fame's Odyssey (Ch. Weylin Willie of Whitehall ex Ch. Fame of Marcmora) owned and bred by W. J. and S. L. Peacy,

stood out in this class of very worthy champions. He caught my eye immediately and on closer acquaintance did not disappoint me. He was just what I would want were I to search the world over for an Irish Wolfhound to show and breed from.

Mrs. Sheila Kemp, Witchesbroom Kennels, formerly West Sussex, England, now Canada, sounded a more pointed warning after judging the Irish Wolfhound Association of the Delaware Valley (IWADV) Specialty show in 1988:

There was some excellent stock in Delaware Valley, but I regret to report that the quality in general was disappointing. . . . We show blocky-headed, short-legged dogs as if our interest was to breed scent-hounds not sighthounds. Substance is either celebrated (especially in bitches) to the point of coarseness or so wanting (especially in dogs) that one fears more for the hunter than the hunted. But what is lacking most of all is stock not simply of great size and commanding appearance but stock combining both these attributes with Grey-hound-like proportions.

This is a problem of type which, in my opinion, is the major problem confronting us today. The problem of type challenges us to explain, or perhaps more relevant, guard against a state of confusion which celebrates diversity over unity. As judges we compile ever more detailed lists of faults, but I fear while we may be winning the occasional battle, we are losing the war. Current diversity of type in our breed is simply too great.

Integral to this problem is the degree to which we have strayed from the Greyhound heritage of our breed. Irish Wolfhounds are supposed to be remarkable for combining power and swiftness with keen sight because they are supposed to be the largest of the sighthounds. . . . In 1927, J. F. Bailey put it this way: "To produce a dog of great power built on galloping, i.e., Greyhound, lines has been the difficulty so far, but it should not be insurmountable."

As breeders, we all know how easy it is to seduce ourselves into believing that what we are currently breeding is just fine, that our most recent litter is the best ever, that it is other people's stock, not ours, that deviates from the Standard. But if we are to accept Bailey's invitation to surmount the problem of type, we must contemplate the Standard of Excellence as a whole and breed accordingly.

Despite these words of warning, Mrs. Kemp found a number of dogs with correct type. Of her Best of Breed, Ch. Bearflag Skeagh (Bearflag Magmellan Seneschal ex Keystone Ksan), bred by Jack and Judi Orsi and owned by Deirdre and Leslie Pitteway, Mrs. Kemp said:

> I was struck by the nobility of this lovely sound bitch. A well-constructed animal with good front assembly, good tuck-up and arch over the loin. Nice bone, good feet, powerful hindquarters with low set hocks. She has a powerful arched neck, a rarity. A credit to her owners and breeders.

Mrs. Kemp also noted several other hounds who possessed correct type. For example, she wrote that the Winners Bitch, Stoneybrook Sovryn (Ch. Sepulcur Shamus ex Meadowbrook Minnewashta), owned and bred by Lynn and Judy Simon, was "extremely well-balanced and in hard condition with *Greyhoundlike proportions* [emphasis added] displaying both correct topline and underline."

We must not rest on our laurels, but neither must we fall into an equally dangerous state, in which we demand perfection from living things. Breeding Irish Wolfhounds to correct type, that is, balancing power and speed in a Greyhound-like form, will always elude us, in the absolute sense. But if we keep in our mind's eye the ancient breed, and realize how fragile is the balance between the ancient stock and the crossbreeding done to save it, we will never again reach the precipice that Graham faced more than a century ago, and that we approached, and narrowly avoided again, twenty years ago.

The Empty Chair

4

"Gentle Giants": Irish Wolfhound Character

No other dog can come so close to the understanding and kindly companionship that exists between humans as this dog can. A giant in structure, a lamb in disposition, a lion in courage; affectionate and intelligent, thoroughly reliable and dependable at all times, as a companion and as a guard he is perfection.
—Joseph A. McAleenan, early in the twentieth century

IRISH WOLFHOUNDS with true Irish Wolfhound character make a profound impression on all who see them. I saw my first Irish Wolfhound at Sanctuary Kennels, an unforgettable experience. As we drove up, I looked ahead and saw six Irish Wolfhounds, heads held high, with beautiful faces, looking at us with the most expressive eyes I have ever seen in a dog. No wonder that so many have noted the beautiful heads of the Sanctuary hounds. These majestic dogs stood nearly motionless, except for their slowly wagging tails. In stark contrast, in the kennel opposite the Irish Wolfhounds were a group of Pomeranians who jumped wildly about, barking and in general demanding our attention. My attention was riveted on the Wolfhounds.

We had with us a small boy who was terrified of dogs. The dogs towered over him. Miss May Atfield, who lived then with Miss Margaret Harrison, proprietress of Sanctuary Kennels, coaxed the boy into Ch. Sanctuary Brave Knight's (Ch. Rory of Kihone ex Kilfenora of Ouborough) kennel. Terrified, the boy finally entered with Miss Atfield. Brave Knight stood quietly; within minutes the boy had lost his fear, and laughingly accepted Brave Knight's licking. That is Irish Wolfhound character at its best. That day I decided I had to have an Irish Wolfhound. My wife agreed. We bought the first one available from Sanctuary Kennels, Sanctuary Peggeen. I have never been without an Irish Wolfhound since. I can't imagine life without one.

Many have attempted to capture the essence of Irish Wolfhound character in words and phrases, including "Gentle when stroked, fierce when provoked," "silent sufferers," "gentle giant," "fragile," "dignified," "noble," "natural rugged beauty." All these phrases, and others similar to them, I have frequently heard longtime owners and breed experts use when describing the Irish Wolfhound's character. Before you get an Irish Wolfhound, you should learn much more than the initial powerful impression they make.

LATE MATURITY AND EARLY DEATH

Two sad but universal characteristics all owners must live with: Irish Wolfhounds mature late and die young. A very few reach ten or more years; many die before they are five. Most will die by seven. Gretchen Bernardi published a study of Irish Wolfhound mortality and morbidity, the first truly empirical study of its kind, which reported the following findings:

> ... in this study of 582 Irish Wolfhounds (291 males, 274 females [sex of 17 unknown]) in the United States that died between January 1, 1966, and January 1, 1986, the mean age at time of death for all dogs was 6.47 years (6.0 years for males, 6.55 years for females). The leading cause of death was cancer, with osteogenic sarcoma being the principal cause of cancer. The causes of death, the incidence of each and the percentage of the total number of dogs in this study are:
>
> 1. Cardiovascular Disease (88 or 15.1%)
> 2. Cancer (197 or 33.9%)

Ch. Major Acres Branwyn, F.Ch. (Ch. Major Acres Vanguard ex Ch. Major Acres Fannee Manahan), a magnificent veteran, pictured here at age ten!

3. Arthritis (30 or 5.2%)
4. Gastric Dilitation Volvulus (68 or 11.7%)
5. Poisoning (1 or .17%)
6. Bacterial Infection (30 or 5.2%)
7. Viral Disease (9 or 1.6%)
8. Trauma (21 or 3.6%)
9. Intestinal Blockage (8 or 1.4%)
10. Post-Surgical Complications (5 or .86%)
11. Kidney Disease (24 or 4.1%)
12. Liver Disease (10 or 1.7%)
13. Euthanized Due to Poor Temperament (6 or 1.0%)
14. Deaths from Various Other Causes (37 or 6.4%)
15. Deaths from Unknown Causes (48 or 8.3%)

Mrs. Bernardi commented on the effects of the short life span of Irish Wolfhounds on owners:

> A few respondents, former owners, commented strongly that, while they loved the breed and enjoyed the time that they had spent with them, they would never again own one, because the sorrow involved in losing these dogs was too great. But many more people took the time to write that they would continue to live with these dogs despite their short lives. It is surely a testament to the great appeal of this breed that so many people continue to own them through what is often great adversity.

Anyone contemplating owning an Irish Wolfhound must consider this fundamental fact of Irish Wolfhound life.

Puppyhood and youth consume most of an Irish Wolfhound's life. The hound remains a puppy for a good year and a half, continues to be immature until well beyond two, lives as a young adult until three or more, probably in most cases not reaching its prime until at least four or five. Most Irish Wolfhounds live only about a quarter of their lives in their prime and beyond. Fortunately, most Irish Wolfhounds experience short declining old age. Most will decline quickly following their prime. Commonly, I hear owners say, "She was fine until about a week ago, then she seemed to weaken almost before my eyes." Recently, one of my bitches died at eight. Not a week before, I looked at her, thought she never looked better, and decided I would show her as a veteran. The next day, I noticed a slight sway to her back, and within four days she looked like an old, dying dog—which she was. I put her down, only seven days after deciding she looked good enough to show!

L. O. Starbuck with Ch. Killabrick. Whelped in July 1927, Killabrick was out of Ch. Mona of Ambleside and sired Ch. Brannish of Ambleside, Ambleside Finn of Erin, Kilshane of Ambleside, Padraic of Summerhill, Ch. Killary of Ambleside, and Ch. Gartha of Ambleside.

SILENT SUFFERERS

Irish Wolfhounds do not complain; Mrs. Nagle called them "silent sufferers." They are. You must be ever vigilant, looking for signs of injury or illness. Mrs. Elzer learned that her Ch. Keystone's Garda Siocana Doc, Winners Dog and Best of Winners at the 1972 IWCA Specialty, was terminally ill only because he would not lie down to sleep. She discovered he had advanced cancer in his chest, had difficulty breathing, hence could not breathe comfortably while reclining. Never a complaint, however, from Doc, even though he was dying. Minutes before Witchesbroom Maffiossi (Ch. Witchesbroom Wizard ex Sulhamstead Medley) died, he weakly nudged an attendant and wagged his tail at the hospital. I had a puppy with a broken leg who never cried with pain; he simply would not walk on it. Ch. Garda Siocana Keystone Kes (Ch Keystone Ko-op ex Ch. Rathrahilly Im Garda Siocana) had an enormous malignant tumor in her neck that spread throughout her body. Although she could barely breathe, she never complained, and remained affectionate until I put her down.

CREATURES OF HABIT

Irish Wolfhounds are creatures of habit. Once either they develop or you impose a routine, Irish Wolfhounds will maintain it, rigidly. They want to enter and exit through the same gates, in the same manner, every time. They want to follow the same paths through the areas familiar to them. They will get up in the same way, lie down in the same way, in fact do all the everyday things they do—day in, day out—without alteration. Owners who observe their hounds even casually quickly learn their patterns, quickly noticing any deviation from these patterns.

Experienced owners know they cannot ignore these deviations. Perhaps they mean nothing. Sometimes, however, a break in habit signals a problem, usually illness or injury, or something else amiss. I never ignore my hounds' deviation from their rigid behavior patterns. Usually, the deviation means nothing, but I have never regretted checking it out. If nothing is wrong, I am reassured; if they are ill or injured, then I can take care of it—sometimes. Once Ch. Meadowbrook King Arthur (Ch. Garda Siocana Keystone Kilty ex

This is Darragh. *Dana Steichen*

Ch. Keystone Kilkerry) and his littermate Meadowbrook Sir Lance-lot (Best of Breed, IWCA Specialty 1978) did not jump up to greet me when I came in the room. I called to them; they rose slowly—a characteristic of some older dogs, but never had these two yearlings acted this way. My veterinarian, then not experienced in Wolfhound ways, assured me nothing was wrong. However, within hours they had raging fevers (106°F), which a return trip to my veterinarian revealed to be caused by pneumonia, not even detectable a few hours before. Fortunately, penicillin quickly killed the bacterial infection, and they made a complete recovery.

A word of advice to novices: Don't be an alarmist and take extreme measures every time your hound does not respond in pre-cisely the same way. Use common sense. If your hound breaks a habit, check it out. Usually, this means investigating whether this deviation constitutes an inexplicable quirk that means nothing. I usually call to them, or do something to determine if they will respond normally to another ordinary situation. For example, if a hound *always* gets up when you come in the room (some do, others do not), but on this occasion does not, then arrange to provoke some other response you know always takes place. For example, if your hound always jumps up when you remove the food dish, try moving the food dish. If your hound jumps up, everything is fine. If not, continue to watch for irregular activities for a short while.

If your hound does not start responding and behaving normally within a reasonable time—"reasonable" probably means a few hours unless things turn drastically worse—then check with your vet. My vet, now that he knows Irish Wolfhounds well, advises that it is better to be safe than sorry. He knows that what may mean nothing in other breeds could spell great danger in Irish Wolfhounds. In fact, he believes that vets should take special courses in school on Irish Wolfhounds because the rules for other breeds simply do not apply to Irish Wolfhounds. None of this means you should watch your dog constantly, looking for breaks in routine. Nor does it mean that you run to the vet every time some little break occurs. If either of these were necessary, then who would want an Irish Wolfhound? It simply means that you should notice your dog's changes in habit. They may mean nothing—they usually do; they could, however, signal danger.

The great Sulhamstead Major (Sulhamstead ex Ch. Sulhamstead Morna of Eaglescrag) at age three and a half, just before his prime.

Ch. Tyrone of Ballykelly (Casey of Ballykelly ex Ch. Antostal of Ballykelly) was bred in Ireland by Sheelagh Seale and owned by Barbara O'Neill. Tyrone won the IWCA trophy for the most Group placements in 1960.   *Rudolph W. Tauskey*

GENTLE GIANTS

Short-lived, late-maturing, silent-suffering creatures of habit—not too promising, you might reasonably respond. In learning about Irish Wolfhound character, however, we must, as in all things, take the bad with the good. The good, in my judgment, outweighs the bad. One remarkable dimension to breed character lies in the extraordinary way in which Irish Wolfhounds manage their extraordinary physical power. Make no mistake about it, they could catch us and dispatch us quickly enough if they chose. Many Sulhamstead hounds proved that to me when I walked them. Once, determined that Sulhamstead Major would not get the best of me, I wrapped the end of his thick leather lead around me, and grabbed the rest with both my hands. When he decided to go *his* way, I threw all my weight in the opposite direction—he snapped the lead with what seemed no effort, ran off about twenty-five yards, turned and looked at me flat on the ground, then ran back and licked me all over the face. Watch your hound demolish large beef shinbones, or open its mouth and consider those powerful jaws. They could snap your neck instantly. But how gently Irish Wolfhounds deal with your hand in their mouths. It may be true in human affairs, as Lord Acton said, that power corrupts, and absolute power corrupts absolutely. Fortunately, Lord Acton's brilliant aphorism does not apply to Irish Wolfhounds.

DIGNITY AND COURAGE

This virtual total restraint on their enormous power bears directly on Irish Wolfhound temperament, another critical dimension to breed character. Most Irish Wolfhounds I have encountered, whether here or in England, not only accept but also want affection from every person they encounter. Some people, reasonably I think, believe that this detracts from their essential dignity, their "great size and commanding appearance." I remember Miss Harrison, Sanctuary Kennels, commenting on Irish Wolfhounds as guard dogs. She said, "If their size does not put the burglar off, then you're lost, and probably your hound as well because he will probably follow the burglar, whom he will treat as a happily newfound companion, right out of your own home!"

A beautiful Veteran Bitch, Witchesbroom Cauldron (Eng. Ch. Witchesbroom Wizard ex Witchesbroom Magic), at eight years.

Gemmah of Bokra (Eng. Ch. Witchesbroom Wizard ex Chicanery of Bokra), a Veteran Bitch filled with quality and type at eight-and-a-half years.

I have owned two mildly protective hounds; neither harmed anyone, although many times they easily could have done so. I have had many people tell me that however friendly my dogs are when I am around, they would not be so if I were not present. I don't believe this for a minute, but I always allow strangers to think whatever they wish, despite what I know the truth to be. Some Irish Wolfhounds do not seem to crave attention so universally. These appeal to some people; perhaps they even fit the ideal Irish Wolfhound type better than do the more uncritically affectionate hounds. Consistent with the Standard's description "of great size and commanding appearance," Irish Wolfhounds probably *should* need, let alone display, less dependence on all humans who come within their range.

An early-nineteenth-century English observer, Mrs. L. S. Hall, at the time a well-known author, captured the ideal Irish Wolfhound character in the following description, based on an Irish Wolfhound, Bruno, whom she knew when she was a child:

> He was the property of an old friend of my grandmother's who claimed descent from the Irish kings. His name was O'Toole; his manners were the most courtly you can imagine. His visits were my jubilees. There was the kind, dignified, old gentleman who told me tales, and there was his tall gaunt dog, grey with age, yet with me full of play. There were two terriers &c., &c. O'Toole and his dogs always occupied the same room, the terriers on the same bed as their master. No entreaty, however, would induce Bruno to sleep on anything softer than stone. He would remove the hearthrug and lie on the marble. His master used to instance the dog's disdain of luxury as a mark of his noble nature. The O'Tooles had three of these dogs. I can recall nothing more picturesque than that majestic old gentleman and his dog, both remnants of a bygone age. Bruno was rough, but not long-coated—very grave, observant, enduring everyone, very fond of children, playing with them gently, but only crouching and fawning on his master; and that, O'Toole would say, "is proof of my royal blood."

The largest Irish Wolfhound I ever bred—taller than 36 inches, weighing at least 175 pounds—saw a mother and her two small children, both toddlers, about a hundred yards away. He stood erect, in that wonderful gazehound stance when spying something of interest. He was not on lead; I was anxious; his owners, novices to Irish Wolfhounds, were not. When the dog broke into a gallop toward the trio, the owners said, "Watch what he does." At about three feet from the mother and the small children, he came to an abrupt stop, approached with amazing gentleness, and stood until the small chil-

Hounds Old and New at Gettysburg

Bev Stobart

dren walked toward him. He slowly wagged his tail, but otherwise did not move. Soon the children, gingerly at first, then gleefully, touched and hugged that gigantic hound.

This was an impressive, but wholly typical, display of ideal Irish Wolfhound restraint in the exercise of its power. Nonetheless, I cautioned these owners against permitting this kind of behavior with strangers. However gentle the hound, these were unique strangers not to get frightened at this enormous dog's galloping approach. To make my point, I told them about an experience I had had. I used to go out with Sulhamstead Felix early in the morning when I believed no one was about. One morning, before dawn, he and I were running when suddenly he stopped, alerted by something I didn't see. Before I could get to him, he broke into a gallop and came upon a middle-aged man jogging in the park. It terrified the man, even though Felix stopped short of contact with him and stood wagging his tail waiting for the man's attention. The man's terror soon turned to fury, which he vented on me—quite appropriately, I add. This man didn't know what this powerful dog lunging at him out of the dark might do! Appearances, not reality, govern our reactions in such situations.

NEVER WITH THEIR TAILS BETWEEN THEIR LEGS

To return to the point—both the reserved and openly affectionate hounds fall within the range of acceptable Irish Wolfhound temperament. Aggressive or shy hounds, however, are clearly beyond the pale. Both characteristics flout the Standard, and aggressiveness endangers human life. Fortunately, aggressiveness is rare in our breed. When it arises, owners must take drastic action—they must destroy the dog. They must also notify their dog's breeder immediately. I have bred one aggressive dog; I hope I never breed another. The man bought a puppy from me and took him home at twelve weeks. He treated the dog as his equal, wrestling and otherwise roughhousing with him. The dog responded in kind. As the hound grew older, he occasionally growled at his owner. The man thought little of it until the dog got territorial about parts of the house, not permitting his owner to enter freely.

Finally, when the dog almost injured him, the man called me to ask my advice. I did not hesitate. I told him, "Destroy the dog. He is a danger to you and to others, and he discredits his breed." I

"Gentle When Stroked"

Berwyck's Mavis enjoying the snow at eleven years of age.

agreed to let the man take his dog to a dog behaviorist at the University of Minnesota before he put him down. The dog behaved fine away from home. Obviously enough, he felt "territorial" only on *his* territory, and rivalry only with *his* owner. The behaviorist confirmed this. The man blamed himself for not establishing the proper relationship with his hound. The behaviorist agreed with him. It would have been easy to accept that explanation; I did not. Rearing may have nurtured the aggressiveness, but it must have been present always, lying there beneath the surface, waiting for the right circumstance, or combination of circumstances, to bring it out. Remember, the true Irish Wolfhound *never* abuses the enormous, deadly if you will, power that it possesses. Owners and breeders alike must accept their custodial responsibility to destroy aggressive hounds in order to preserve the integrity of the breed and to protect the people they may frighten and injure.

More prevalent and less dangerous, shy dogs flout the Standard's "commanding appearance." Furthermore, they cause both their owners and themselves pain and suffering. It always causes anguish to their owners and to those who know Irish Wolfhound character to see these gigantic dogs with their tails between their legs, terrified at the approach of any stranger, cowering as they draw near, crashing into their owners, and even crashing through plate-glass doors to escape strangers. These pathetic hounds, except when either alone or around people they know well and trust, live fearful and desperate lives. I have lived with one shy hound; I will never live with another. She was a loving, devoted bitch who was happy as long as no strangers drew near. I can remember how she enjoyed riding in the car, but how quickly her joy turned to fear when she encountered strangers too close to the car.

On one occasion, a man stopped at a traffic light next to us, reached, perhaps a bit too quickly, toward this bitch, while expressing to me his admiration for Irish Wolfhounds. She pulled back, shrinking onto the backseat of the car until he disappeared at the light's change. I told the man in the seconds I had how Irish Wolfhounds should not be shy. Celeste Hutton had one of these shy dogs. When someone commented that the bitch had improved because the woman's approach did not "freak out" the bitch, Celeste said nothing. When the woman walked away, Celeste turned to me and said, "I didn't have the nerve to tell her that the poor bitch didn't move because she was literally frozen with fear." Celeste was right, as any experienced owner knows. Her muscles were taut; you could see the

Members of the family: Ch. Keystone Kilkerry and Ch. Garda Siocana Keystone Kilty, sire and dam to Meadowbrook Sir Lancelot, Best of Breed, Best of Winners, 1978 IWCA Specialty.

Mrs. Nagle, Sulhamstead Kennels, at home with her two last champions, Ch. Sepulcur Meg of Sulhamstead, and Ch. Lainston Laodamia of Sulhamstead.

whites of her eyes; she stood rigidly next to her owner; and, most telltale, she had her tail between her legs. Some say that Irish Wolfhounds put their tails between their legs for a number of reasons; I do not accept this for a minute. Down through the ages, the phrase "tail between his legs" has meant only one thing. When you see it in an Irish Wolfhound, you *know* that something frightens or disturbs that dog.

Great controversy rages over what constitutes shyness, what causes it, and how we should respond to it. At one extreme, some maintain that any dog that does not eagerly seek contact with everyone is shy. At the other extreme are those who argue that only Irish Wolfhounds who will not approach strangers or who actively avoid any contact with them are shy. Although most Irish Wolfhounds are extremely outgoing, I do not believe that anything less constitutes shyness. In fact, it is perfectly acceptable, probably desirable, and surely consistent with the basic character of Irish Wolfhounds, to hesitate in the presence of strangers, certainly to withhold effusive affection from them. To hesitate and withhold effusive affection is one thing. Irish Wolfhounds, however, should never react to the mere *presence* of strangers in any other way. The hound who "freaks out" by pulling away or crashing into its owner or cowering in a corner in a stranger's presence, is a shy Irish Wolfhound. Of course, a stranger who brandishes a club, lurches toward the dog, or otherwise behaves in a threatening manner, might provoke something more than hesitation. However, I have not seen stable Irish Wolfhounds so react, even in the face of such provocation.

Two basic theories, and that is what they are—theories—because no one has empirically demonstrated the truth of either, have been advanced to explain the causes of shyness. The environmentalists contend that either some event, usually in a "critical" stage of the dog's life, or some deficiency in diet, or some combination of both, causes shyness. I have heard owners tell many stories about a traumatic event during "adolescence" (usually somewhere between five months and one year old) that caused their dog to become shy, or "nervous" as the English say. Prior to the event, the dog was fine; forever after it was shy. I could multiply variations on these stories almost ad infinitum, since I have heard so many of them.

All these stories have the following common elements: (1) the dog was outgoing prior to the incident; (2) then a man—Irish Wolfhounds rarely shy from women—approached, or moved, or wore a particular item of clothing, or did not shave (for some reason beards

104

Drakesleat Irish Wolfhounds, owned by Zena Andrews, England. From right to left: Ch. Iseult, Ch. Barvyck, Ch. Sovryn, Kryn, and Ch. Tokyn.

seem to especially bother shy Irish Wolfhounds), or in some other manner aroused the dog's suspicion; (3) the dog shied away from men for the rest of its life. I don't doubt the truth of these stories, first because the people who have told them to me are credible, honorable people, and second because I have witnessed it. I had a bitch who was outgoing and who never hesitated in the presence of strangers. Then, when she was eight months old, a large, overbearing man lunged toward her, shouting in a loud voice, "Hi, girl, how are you!" and slapped her on the side. He meant well; he loved dogs. She "freaked out," running to the corner of the room where she cowered until he left, no matter how I tried to coax her to move. No man could ever approach her after that.

Others maintain that vitamin and mineral deficiencies, particularly in the central nervous system, produce shyness. They argue that correcting these deficiencies, usually by adding vitamin-mineral supplements to the diet, will eliminate shyness. I know of no *convincing empirical* evidence proving that vitamin and mineral supplements reduce or eliminate shyness in Irish Wolfhounds. I have heard *impressionistic evidence* from people who adamantly maintain that they have witnessed the beneficial results of vitamin, mineral, and other dietary therapy in their own hounds or in hounds they know well.

The hereditarians argue that Irish Wolfhounds inherit the *tendency* to shyness; events merely provide the occasion for this hereditary tendency to manifest itself. In other words, the dog has a basic "weakness" of temperament that a frightening event, usually during "adolescence," causes to break through into open behavior. More specifically, strangers, particularly men who behave or appear "odd" or different, cause Irish Wolfhounds with a tendency toward shyness to become shy. It only looks like the event caused the shyness. It did, of course, but only in the most superficial way.

One talented vet of the hereditarian school put it this way. If a sadist beats a basically stable Irish Wolfhound for three weeks straight, that Irish Wolfhound may rightly cower and shy from strangers—*for a while.* However, once in the presence of trustworthy, kind people, the Irish Wolfhound will return to "normal," accepting warmly, or at least not "spooking" at the sight of, strangers. The scars of maltreatment will heal in the Irish Wolfhound of basically sound temperament; the event will permanently alter only an Irish Wolfhound with a hereditary tendency to shyness, according to this vet.

Owners report how mistreated hounds gladly accepted strang-

Kinsale of Boroughbury, owned by Thomas B. Wannamaker, Jr., was Winners Bitch at the 1951 Specialty under Esther M. Croucher held at Harbor Cities.
Joan Ludwig

At the 1955 IWCA Specialty, judging honors fell to the legendary all-breed authority Alva Rosenberg. His choice for Best of Breed was Ch. Tralee of Ambleside (right), owned by Charles H. Morse, Jr., and handled by Virginia Hardin. Best of Opposite Sex was Ch. The McGillacudy, owned by Clyde B. Smith.
William Brown

ers once they were back in a healthy environment for a reasonable length of time. They also report—and I have owned—Irish Wolfhounds who bounced quickly back to "normal" following a single startling experience. One bitch shied away from Mrs. Jenkins when she judged Irish Wolfhounds in Philadelphia at the IWCA Specialty in 1976—the bitch had never shied before; she never shied again. Of course, these instances do not constitute unassailable empirical proof that shyness is hereditary, but they suggest that heredity may well explain why some hounds react permanently to one frightening incident, while others return to normal soon after the incident, or after mistreatment ceases.

Hilary Jupp, careful student of the Irish Wolfhound, told me once, "There is no point in producing magnificent specimens of the breed that are either so aggressive that they are dangerous to live with [or] so nervous that their lives are a misery of fear." Rosemary Follett (Ederyn Kennels, England), breeder and international judge, said the Irish Wolfhound "should be respected as a calm, gentle animal of dignity, and as a companion to humans." Only the tall, Greyhound-like, dignified hound who suffers pain silently, never abuses its enormous power, responds to virtually all situations unflappingly, and never appears shy, shrinking, or frightened without reason can meet the Irish Wolfhound Standard's prime mandate to be "of great size and commanding appearance." Only such a hound reflects true Irish Wolfhound character. Only that character can fill its owner with the pride, joy, and continuing satisfaction that *typical* Irish Wolfhounds provide.

5

The Fundamental Law of Breed Type: The Official Irish Wolfhound Standard

General Appearance—Of great size and commanding appearance, the Irish Wolfhound is remarkable in combining power and swiftness with keen sight. The largest and tallest of the galloping hounds, in general type he is a rough-coated Greyhoundlike breed; very muscular, strong though gracefully built; movements easy and active; head and neck carried high, the tail carried with an upward sweep with a slight curve towards the extremity. The minimum height and weight of dogs should be 32 inches and 120 pounds; of bitches, 30 inches and 105 pounds; these to apply only to hounds over 18 months of age. Anything below this should be debarred from competition. Great size, including height at shoulder and proportionate length of body, is the desideratum to be aimed at, and it is desired to firmly establish a race that shall average from 32 to 34 inches in dogs, showing the requisite power, activity, courage and symmetry.

Head—Long, the frontal bones of the forehead very slightly raised and very little indentation between the eyes. Skull, not too broad. Muzzle, long and moderately pointed. Ears, small and Greyhoundlike in carriage.

Neck—Rather long, very strong and muscular, well arched, without dewlap or loose skin about the throat.

Chest—Very deep. Breast, wide.

Back—Rather long than short. Loins, arched.

Tail—Long and slightly curved, of moderate thickness, and well covered with hair.

Belly—Well drawn up.

Forequarters—Shoulders muscular, giving breadth of chest, set sloping. Elbows well under, neither turned inwards nor outwards.

Leg—Forearm muscular, and the whole leg strong and quite straight.

Hindquarters—Muscular thighs and second thighs long and strong as in the Greyhound, and hocks well let down and turning neither in nor out.

Feet—Moderately large and round, neither turned inwards nor outwards. Toes, well arched and closed. Nails, very strong and curved.

Hair—Rough and hard on body, legs and head; especially wiry and long over eyes and under jaw.

Color and Markings—The recognized colors are gray, brindle, red, black, pure white, fawn, or any other color that appears in the Deerhound.

Faults—Too light or heavy a head, too highly arched frontal bone; large ears and hanging flat to the face; short neck; full dewlap; too narrow or broad a chest; sunken or hollow or quite straight back; bent forelegs; overbent fetlocks; twisted feet; spreading toes; too curly a tail; weak hindquarters and a general want of muscle; too short in body; lips or nose liver-colored or lacking in pigmentation.

LIST OF POINTS IN ORDER OF MERIT

Points.

1. Typical.
2. Great size and commanding appearance.
3. Movements easy and active.
4. Head, long and level, carried high.

5. Forelegs, heavily boned, quite straight, elbows well set under.
6. Thighs long and muscular; second thighs, well muscled, stifles nicely bent.
7. Coat, rough and hard, specially wiry and long over eyes and under jaw.
8. Body, long, well ribbed up, with ribs well sprung, and great breadth across hips.
9. Loins arched, belly well drawn up.
10. Ears, small with Greyhoundlike carriage.
11. Feet, moderately large and round, toes, close, well arched.
12. Neck, long, well arched and very strong.
13. Chest, very deep, moderately broad.
14. Shoulders, muscular, set sloping.
15. Tail, long and slightly curved.
16. Eyes, dark.

Note—The above in no way alters the "Standard of Excellence," which must in all cases be rigidly adhered to; they simply give the various points in order of merit. If in any case they appear at variance with Standard of Excellence, it is the latter which is correct.

Approved September 12, 1950

These powerful nineteenth-century Greyhounds were what Captain Graham had in mind when he called the Irish Wolfhound Greyhound-like.

6

A Discussion of Breed Type: A Gloss on the Standard

$\mathbf{T}$HE IRISH WOLFHOUND STANDARD is the Constitution, the fundamental law of our breed. Breeders, in selecting stud dogs and brood bitches to mate, in choosing puppies to keep and dogs to exhibit, must comply with its commands. Officially, judges must place dogs and award prizes according to it. Like all laws, the practices of breeders and judges do not always reflect the words of the Standard. In the first place, most of the words of the Standard require interpretation; they do not capture precisely the framers' meaning. In order to understand what those who wrote the Standard meant by such phrases as "great size," "commanding appearance," "back—rather long than short," and others, we need to study the history of the breed and scrutinize the descriptions, verbal and graphic, that the founders and their descendants have left us. Samples of both appear throughout this book.

Like all human expression, the Standard cannot perfectly communicate its authors' meaning to those who study its language. Even

Ch. Sulhamstead Max (Ch. Sulhamstead Fellus ex Ch. Sulhamstead Mystic), an outstanding hound that appears in many quality hounds' pedigrees. Note the beautiful head carriage and the flow of the neckline into the body. Bred and owned by Mrs. F. Nagle, Sulhamstead Kennels.

Saragh of Eaglescrag (Ch. Sulhamstead Sedelstan Rebel ex Song of Eaglescrag). Note the lovely arch over the loin, and overall type. Bred and owned by Mr. and Mrs. L. S. Jenkins, Eaglescrag Kennels, Wales.

if the drafters make their meaning clear, reasonable people can—and do—differ over what the Standard means, because individual perceptions and understandings differ. Honest people can read the same words and understand them differently, can look at the same pictures and see different things. This should not lead to the conclusion that everyone's interpretation of the Standard is equal. Most emphatically not! Mrs. Keith Follett, Ederyn Kennels, put it well when she wrote: "The Standard . . . paints a picture that is difficult to better. Not *my* type or *your* type, or the type of any particular kennel, but conforming to a standard of excellence to produce hounds that could hunt and despatch a wolf. . . ."

Interpreting the Standard demands two qualifications: (1) the gift called "an eye for a dog," namely, the innate capacity to recognize quality, joined with (2) the requisite knowledge to interpret the Standard. Few possess this knowledge, but most can acquire it if they take the time and make the effort. Effort can *develop* the untrained, undisciplined eye; it can never *create* an eye. Only nature confers that gift. True breeders and worthy judges must possess both nature's gift of an "eye for a dog" and the requisite knowledge to develop that eye. These breeders and judges know what to look for in an Irish Wolfhound, and they recognize it instantly when they see it. All, however, can benefit greatly from studying the provisions in the Standard, which requires first a very careful examination of the words themselves.

The gloss, or elaboration on the Standard's provisions, follows language in the Standard as it appears. The discussion, photographs, and the sketches draw together from a wide variety of sources some of the impressive record of knowledge surrounding the Irish Wolfhound Standard. I have tried to organize and present this knowledge in a fashion that novices, prospective judges, and even experienced breeders might find useful, and hopefully even provocative. Some of the material has never been published. Most of it is a synthesis of what I have learned over the past twenty years observing, reading about, breeding, and judging Irish Wolfhounds here, in Canada, and in England.

The discussion leans heavily on the knowledge of others. Some of that knowledge comes from books and articles far too long out of print, and inaccessible to all but the most diligent students. Much of it I have gleaned from listening, I hope carefully and attentively, if not always obediently, to the late Mrs. Florence Nagle, Sulhamstead Kennels; Mrs. L. S. Jenkins, Eaglescrag Kennels; Miss Susan Hudson, Brabyns Kennels in England; and the late Mrs. C. Groverman Ellis and Miss Mary Jane Ellis, Killybracken Kennels in the United States. I have tried to follow the sequence of the Standard in the gloss. Captain Graham made valuable comments on each part of the English Standard. I have not paraphrased Captain Graham; the last word, where he spoke it, should be his alone.

That the Standard requires elaboration should not suggest that it needs modification. Today, as several times in the past, a move is afoot to alter the Standard, to bring it into compliance with a template designed by the American Kennel Club. The enormous numbers of dogs, the huge entries at dog shows, and the ignorance of so many judges, have all contributed to this recent threat to the integrity of the Irish Wolfhound Standard. Somehow, the "reformers" believe, simply reordering, rephrasing, and, make no mistake, modifying the Standard's content, will give judges a step-by-step guide to judging dogs. If all Standards follow the same pattern, the reformers maintain, judging will proceed more smoothly, more effectively, and more harmoniously. As if uniformity can improve quality; in fact, it invites mediocrity, shelters ignorance, and nourishes incompetence.

The shortcomings in the Irish Wolfhound Standard arise out of the unavoidable and unalterable imperfection of all human endeavors, particularly transforming a mind's eye picture of the ideal Irish Wolfhound into printed words. The Standard's language stands as strong testimony to how close its authors came to overcoming those imperfections. It is a beautiful piece of work, whose genius each careful reading further discloses. I am always amazed when I reread the Standard how it reveals more than prior readings. What appeared vague or inscrutable, even contradictory, becomes clear, understandable, and consistent upon closer study. Whenever the Standard perplexes the reader, I maintain, the fault lies more with the reader than with those who wrote the Standard. Read the Standard and reread it frequently. Study the gloss too and listen to discussion regarding it. But do not rely on these. Return always to the Standard; it is the final word; its wisdom will more than repay your efforts.

The Standard is divided into many parts, but they are intimately related. The General Appearance section refers to the dog as a whole, to the dog's general type, if you will: a dog of great size and commanding appearance, combining power and speed in a Greyhound-like form. The remaining sections state the requirements for the main parts of the dog, literally from head to tail: head, neck,

Ch. Eaglescrag Clonroe of Nendrum (Ch. Sulhamstead Max ex Int. Ch. Carol of Eaglescrag). Note excellent length, sweep, and width of stifle. Bred by Miss N. Twyman, Nendrum Kennels, Ireland; owned by Mr. and Mrs. L. S. Jenkins.

Ch. Chieftan of Brabyns (Feccna of Brabyns ex Petasmeade Chant), whose name appears in the pedigree of many quality dogs. Note the excellent front assembly. Bred by Peta Innes; owned by Miss E. E. S. Hudson, Brabyns Kennels.

forequarters, body, hindquarters, and tail. Each part of the dog, and even the components within those parts, contribute to the General Appearance. Every component of the dog must contribute to the general type. We do not assess head, forequarters, ears, tail, stifles, or any individual part separate from its ultimate purpose—to contribute to type.

One good way to think about the Irish Wolfhound Standard is to keep in mind some other breeds that the Irish Wolfhound resembles, and some the Irish Wolfhound should *not* resemble. The Irish Wolfhound should resemble both the Greyhound and the Scottish Deerhound, but not too much; the Irish Wolfhound should *not* resemble the Great Dane, much less the Mastiff. An important motivating force behind writing the Standard was to specify how closely Irish Wolfhounds should resemble Greyhounds and Scottish Deerhounds, to distinguish them from those two breeds, and to starkly contrast them with Great Danes and Mastiffs. One example will demonstrate this. The Irish Wolfhound Standard calls for small, rose ears, not large ears hanging flat against the skull. Why? Because Greyhounds have small, rose ears; Mastiffs' ears are large, and they hang relatively flat.

During the nineteenth century, when Captain Graham restored the Irish Wolfhound, breeders had not the commitment to breed purity that prevails today. Dogs had functions to perform, and breeders took any dog that performed the function. Only with the onset of breed competition did purebred dogs come into prominence. Captain Graham, therefore, concentrated on purifying the Irish Wolfhound, which entailed removing the Mastiff and Great Dane characteristics. At the same time, he had to strengthen the Greyhound and Deerhound traits while retaining the distinct qualities that typify the Irish Wolfhound.

GENERAL APPEARANCE

(1) Great size, (2) commanding appearance, (3) combining power and speed, in a (4) Greyhound-like form—these four elements compose the essence of Irish Wolfhound type. All the specific parts of the Standard only elaborate upon these fundamental elements. The wisest and most experienced breeders have disagreed over details, but none has disputed these general characteristics as funda-

Ch. Sulhamstead Minstrel (Sulhamstead Woodside Finn ex Ch. Sulhamstead Mica), a hound of quality and sustance. Note the powerful hindquarters, depth of chest, and excellent expression. Bred by Mrs. F. Nagle; owned by Mrs. F. Nagle and Miss M. J. Ellis, Sulhamstead Kennels.

Ch. Solstrand Kaspar (Ch. Marumac Charlock ex Ch. Kellybourne Ice Rocket), a hound of quality, balance, and symmetry. Bred and owned by Mrs. Dagmar Kennis, Solstrand Kennels, England. *Pearce*

mental to Irish Wolfhound type. Captain Graham spoke of General Appearance, or form as he denoted it, in these words:

> That of a very tall, heavy, Scottish Deerhound, much more massive, and very majestic-looking; active and fast, perhaps less so than the present breed of Deerhound.

"Of Great Size"

"Of great size," the Standard begins. *"Coeteris paribus,* size is power,"* wrote the Victorian expert on Greyhounds in Stonehenge's *Dogs of the British Islands.* Size includes both height and length, according to the Standard: "Great size, including height at shoulder and proportionate length of body, is the desideratum to be aimed at." Sadly, too many judges and breeders consider only height, forgetting entirely about length, and although not mentioned, ignoring breadth, size of bone, and amount of muscle. The same Greyhound expert continued after stating the law that size is power:

> But this law must not be taken without exceptions, since there must of necessity be a due proportion of parts, or else the successive actions necessary for speed will not take place . . . because by a well-known mechanical law, what is gained in power is lost in speed or time.

Size, properly conceived in the Irish Wolfhound, embraces (1) height, (2) length, and (3) breadth. (Novices, please note that you determine how tall your dog is at the shoulders, not at the top of the head.) How tall and long is "great?" Does size mean simply tall, or does it encompass length and size of bone and muscle as well? Novices, and incidentally too many experienced fanciers as well, believe that great size means simply height. The Standard, however, calls not only for tall hounds but ones with bone and muscle *proportionate* to height.

Height. The early commentators all referred to the great size of Irish Wolfhounds: Oliver Goldsmith in 1770 said they were "as tall as a calf at a year." Smith, in 1774, said the Irish Wolfhound was "much taller than the Mastiff," the latter itself a large dog. Berwick, in 1790, said the Irish Wolfhound was the "largest of the dog kind." The *Sportsman's Cabinet,* which printed the Reinagle hound (Captain Graham's ideal), in 1804 called the Irish Wolfhound "gigantic." By the nineteenth century, the commentators became more specific

Ch. Antostal Meadhbh Nacenchroe (Ch. Cumin of Killybracken ex Ch. Antostal Mag Eochagain), a beautiful bitch of soft curves and flowing lines. Note the nearly perfect topline. Bred and owned by Miss Gwen Centenno, Antostal Kennel.

Meadowbrook Carol, a graphic study of power in a Greyhound shape. Note the excellent topline, bend of stifle, depth of chest, head and expresson. Bred and owned by J. and J. Samaha, Meadowbrook Kennels.

about height. In 1859, the *Gazetteer of the World* wrote that the Irish Wolfhound was "about three feet" tall.

Throughout history, observers have exaggerated individual hounds' height. James Watson, in his remarkable *Dog Book*, published in 1909, writes that when Mr. Lee and Captain Graham measured Great Danes at the Ranelagh show in 1885, "it was extraordinary how the thirty-five and thirty-six inch animals dwindled down, some of them nearly half a foot at a time." Written more than a century ago about Great Danes, it could as easily refer to claims about Irish Wolfhound height in the 1990s. Owners consistently exaggerate how tall their hounds are. I used to measure my dogs regularly with a wicket a friend made for me. Hence, I *knew* how tall my dogs were. Every time height was mentioned, I would walk near the owner's dog with whatever dog I had. On the average, owners added three to five inches to the their dogs' height. I don't believe they deliberately tried to deceive anyone. They honestly believed what they said.

The Standard demands "great size" and specifies a minimum height of 30 inches for bitches and 32 inches for dogs. It adds that the goal is to establish an *average* height of 32 to 34 inches in dogs and calls for debarring specimens falling below the minimum. Those who wrote the Standard did not want dogs measuring less than 32 inches. (Captain Graham and the English Standard prescribe 31 inches for dogs, 28 for bitches.)

The Standard's language that dogs below the minima should be debarred has no formal effect. No judge can call for the wicket to measure Irish Wolfhounds, nor can judges eject from the ring those they believe fall below those minima. The reason: only Standards that use the word "disqualify" specifically can authorize such action. Hence, the words "should be debarred from competition" cannot disqualify an Irish Wolfhound because it does not reach the prescribed minimum.

Mrs. Nagle frequently used to say, "The Standard calls for 'great size,' but that does not mean the bigger the better." In fact, the Standard surrounds the height requirement with hedges. In specific language, it states that dogs (meaning males) should average between 32 and 34 inches. Of course, this does not mean that hounds that exceed 34 inches automatically depart from type. In fact, they may qualify as exceptionally good hounds, if they meet the second hedge around height alone. In the Standard's words, even dogs 32

Ch. Meadowbrook Lust (Witchesbroom Maffiossi ex Meadowbrook Lady Gwenovere), a bitch of great quality, but lacking in substance, although the picture does not show it. Bred by J. and J. Samaha; owned by Eugenia Barnes and Joel Samaha.

Bold Ruler of Denmar (Ch. Aodh Harp of Eagle ex Ch. Nonesuch Shillelagh), a balanced hound with excellent depth of chest. Bred and owned by L. Gilleaudeau, Nonesuch Kennels.

to 34 inches tall must show "the requisite power, activity, courage and symmetry."

A powerful, energetic, courageous, well-proportioned hound that is 36 inches tall clearly falls within the Standard, perhaps even more desirably so than a 32-inch dog. That is because activity, symmetry, and even sometimes power ordinarily diminish as height increases. We see far too many weak, phlegmatic, narrow, refined tall hounds for the good of the breed. So, although we love to see a 36-inch-tall balanced Irish Wolfhound with "movements easy and active," we rarely do. Furthermore, hounds can reach such a height that they become grotesque. Although not a breed problem, individual hounds too tall for the Standard appear from time to time. Most of them clearly demonstrate the harms associated with too much of a good thing. The reasons for the hedges regarding height lie in focusing our attention on hounds whose height *complements* power, activity, courage, and symmetry but never *replaces* them.

Length. Great size means not only height, it also includes length— "Great size, including height at shoulder *and proportionate length of body*" (emphasis added), commands the Standard. The Standard stresses length throughout: it explicitly calls for a *long* head, a "rather" *long* neck, a back "rather *long* than short," *long* second thighs, and the List of Points in Order of Merit refers to a *long* tail. The authors clearly had length on their minds. "Body and frame lengthy," said Captain Graham. Yet perhaps nothing has stirred up more debate among Irish Wolfhound experts than the Standard's references to length. Just as with height, some inexperienced judges and breeders believe that the longer the dog, the better. No one who knows the history of the breed believes this. They know that Captain Graham and his contemporaries fought against Irish Wolfhounds too short to cover sufficient ground to satisfy the requirement for speed.

The longer the dog, of course, the longer the stride, and consequently the more ground the dog can cover. But these nineteenth-century stock people also knew the basic laws of physics. They knew that what they gained in speed, they lost in power. Hence, to meet the requirement that Irish Wolfhounds combine power and speed, their length must be sufficient to catch a wolf but not so long as to cripple their ability to dispatch the captured quarry. Balance between length and height, that's the key. Of course, the experts will

Ch. Sepulcur Meg of Sulhamstead (Ch. Sulhamstead Motto ex Ch. Sepulcur Meggen), the fiftieth Sulhamstead champion! Bred by Gordon Crane, Sepulcur Kennels; owned by Mrs. F. Nagle.

Ch. Berwyck's Salvation at Caraglen (Ch. Berwyck Mississippi ex Brabyns Finoca). Note the lovely, soft expression, and the far-off look. Bred by Dr. and Mrs. R. Bernardi; owned by Bev and Sue Stobart.

always disagree on exact length, but they do so only within an acceptable spectrum of length and height.

We will return to the subject of length in the gloss on the Standard's requirements concerning the Irish Wolfhound's back. In closing the subject of length in general appearance, it is worth noting that extremists will always push the meaning of the Standard in regard to length to the limit—the longest and tallest dogs are best. This is wrong. It reflects ignorance of the breed's purpose within its historical context, it flouts the laws of physics, and it defies the pervasive search for balance that the Standard mandates.

Breadth. The Standard does not explicitly mention breadth in relation to size, but the subject surely belongs in any discussion of size in the Irish Wolfhound. Extremists in one camp maintain that the thicker the dog the better; other extremists contend that thick means coarse. Everyone agrees that coarseness is anathema. But breadth is not the equivalent of coarseness. Furthermore, coarseness is not a breed problem; refinement definitely is. Disagreement over breadth arises because the Irish Wolfhound must balance power and speed. A dog too narrow lacks strength; a dog too broad lacks speed and grace. Remember, the Standard requires a dog "strong though *gracefully* built" (emphasis added). Too much breadth also impedes the "easy and active" movement the Standard requires. Finally, too much breadth often accompanies short, cobby dogs that resemble Mastiffs, or draft horses if you will, not the "Greyhoundlike breed" that the Standard mandates. So proper breadth, like length, height, and size generally, ultimately depends upon balance.

"Of great size," then, means a dog that has as much height, length, and breadth as is consistent with a "very muscular, strong," "gracefully built," "easy and active[ly]" moving, "Greyhoundlike breed," "remarkable in combining power and swiftness." This combination rules out extremes of any kind—extremely tall, extremely long, and extremely broad!

". . . and Commanding Appearance"

"Having the air or tone of command," says the dictionary under the entry "commanding." Synonyms for "commanding" include "assertive," "authoritative," "masterful," "self-assured," and perhaps best, "imposing." This definition and these synonyms sug-

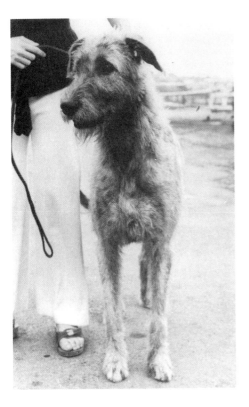

Sanctuary Peggeen (Sanctuary Jayantees Tiberius ex Sanctuary Dornford Boreen). Note the proper shape of legs, and correct feet. Bred by Sanctuary Kennels, England; owned by J. and J. Samaha.

Movement "easy and active." Note the excellent reach in front, and the strong drive from the rear, both of which contribute to the long stride that sets the best-moving Irish Wolfhound apart.

gest four elements in the Standard's requirement of "commanding appearance": (1) physical carriage, (2) temperament, (3) presence or bearing, and (4) quality.

Physical Carriage. The Standard offers this guidance concerning the Irish Wolfhound's physical carriage: "head and neck carried high." Irish Wolfhounds, like all hounds, relied on scent when they hunted. But, like the other sighthounds, they utilized their eyes to discover their quarry. Once sighted, they lowered their heads for more efficient galloping and so that their noses could aid them to keep on course. The initial survey by sight remains in present hounds. Perhaps nothing save the full galloping Irish Wolfhound equals the beauty of an alerted Irish Wolfhound—tall, erect, poised to chase when spying a quarry, or today to appraise anything that attracts its attention.

This beautiful consequence of the performance of a practical function made the Irish Wolfhound a much-desired animal long after the need to hunt wolves disappeared. As early as the eighteenth century, they were kept for their imposing beauty as noted by Oliver Goldsmith, in his *Animated Nature,* published in 1770, and quoted in Chapter 1.

Temperament. The Irish Wolfhound Standard refers to temperament in the General Appearance section, which closes with the phrase "showing the requisite power, activity, courage and symmetry." The key words are "activity" and "courage." The Standard weights temperament heavily. Indeed, without proper temperament, no Irish Wolfhound has "commanding appearance." The dog that fawns over everyone, lying down on its back, wagging its tail, and in short groveling for attention can never have a commanding appearance. I once owned a bitch that literally crawled on her belly to everyone, pleading in a most cloying manner for attention and affection. She reminded me of the Shakespearean character who "made such an ass of himself that he was wondrous to look at, yet I could hardly forebear hurling things at him" (or in this case, her).

Untypical as this groveling, cloying manner is, much worse is the nervous or shy dog that lacks courage and displays fear. It goes without saying that no Irish Wolfhound that cowers behind its owner, or runs and hides, or even simply backs away, rolls its eyes, tenses up, or puts its tail between its legs can ever have a commanding appearance. To put the matter bluntly, both "spooks" and "saps"

128

Ch. Witchesbroom Wild Rose of Drakesleat (Ch. Witchesbroom Wizard ex Witchesbroom Magic), a quality bitch of commanding appearance, made in the Greyhound form. Bred by S. Kemp; owned by Z. Andrews. *Pearce*

Ch. Sepulcur Shamus (Witchesbroom Maffiossi ex Sepulcur Rhea). Notice this Veteran Dog's excellent forechest and overall correct type. Bred by Gordon Crane, Sepulcur Kennels, England; owned by Lynn and Judy Simon.

129

lack an essential element in the Standard's requirement that Irish Wolfhounds exhibit "commanding appearance."

Presence or Bearing. Some beautiful Irish Wolfhounds do not know they are beautiful, or if they do, do not transmit that awareness beyond themselves. This awareness of beauty, and the conveyance of it to all those around, is what we mean by presence or bearing. Mrs. Nagle said an Irish Wolfhound with presence or bearing appears and by the way it carries itself communicates to everyone, "I am the one." They need not "ask" for attention; they do not do so. Their presence alone demands attention, and hence, presence contributes to commanding appearance. In competitions, those with presence and bearing stand away from all the rest. By the same token, beautiful Irish Wolfhounds without presence may win a prize where no competition exists, but never when a hound with presence appears in the same ring. The hound with presence diminishes all those next or near to it.

Quality. Impossible to define adequately, and easy to say what it is not, quality speaks for itself. That excellence or superiority that bespeaks quality may appear in any worldly object or activity. Those who have an eye for quality know it when they see it, even if they cannot put into words what they mean by it, whether in an Irish Wolfhound, an antique, a tennis match, or a student. Sometimes quality accompanies presence, but the two don't always coincide. I have seen hounds of superior quality without presence. One of two Irish Wolfhounds I ever saw that would have deserved the rare adjective "great" had tremendous quality but no presence or bearing because she was shy.

Some consider quality to be in opposition to substance; I have heard older breeders say that a hound has substance but lacks quality, or the opposite—possesses quality without substance. After much thought and effort, I have come up with this concededly woefully inadequate definition of quality in Irish Wolfhounds: quality is that excellence or superiority in symmetry, balance, and soft curves that the best Irish Wolfhounds exhibit.

Ch. Keystone Morlan (Witchesbroom Maffiossi ex Ch. Keystone Kesselring) in his prime.

Ch. Finn Mac Cool of Edgecliff, a Best in Show winner, owned by Edgecliff Kennels.
Joan Ludwig

". . . Remarkable in Combining Power and Swiftness with Keen Sight"

In his monograph *The Irish Wolfhound,* Captain Graham wrote:

> It is not probable that our remote ancestors had any very high standard as to quality or looks. *Strength, stature, and fleetness* [emphasis added] were the points most cultivated.

Captain Graham's pithy, precise, yet graceful statement captures the essence of Irish Wolfhound type—combining power and speed in a huge Greyhound-like frame. Reading those words makes me wonder if it would not serve our breed better to spend time reading the old words rather than devoting energy to writing new ones! In no other respect does the challenge of balance come into bolder relief than in the Standard's mandate to combine power with speed in a large Greyhound-like form. Two reasons account for the fact that we never see Irish Wolfhounds that perfectly combine power and speed. First, no living thing is perfect. Second, the balance between power and speed, as Captain Graham and all who have followed him recognize, is a *precarious* or *delicate* balance, that any slack in vigilance for its achievement upsets.

In the earliest days, two Wolfdogs prevailed, the Greyhound and the Mastiff, according to the Earl of Altamont, whose work is quoted in Chapter 1. Our challenge is to rid the Irish Wolfhound of any hint of the Mastiff without losing the requisite power to dispatch wolves. We can see the Mastiff's influence in the flat ears, broad skulls, short muzzles, large flews, rectangular bodies, and general coarseness in some hounds today.

"Size is power," but "what is gained in power is lost in speed," succinctly wrote the Victorian expert on Greyhounds in Stonehenge's *Dogs of the British Islands.* Even in the Greyhound—the coursing Greyhound like those in Stonehenge—breeders did not totally sacrifice power to speed, although to be sure, speed predominates in the Greyhound. In the Irish Wolfhound, on the other hand, *balance* is the key: to produce a dog in a Greyhound-like form, fast enough to catch a wolf, strong enough to bring it down. Sometimes, of course, in breeding and judging Irish Wolfhounds, we must accept dogs that do not ideally combine swiftness with strength. I believe it is better, when we have to make a choice, that we err on the side

Ch. Ambleside Edain of Edgecliff, a Westminster Best of Breed winner, 1952, owned by Mrs. Starbuck's Ambleside Kennels.

of too much power because the breed tends toward refinement, not coarseness.

All the historical evidence indicates that left to indiscriminate breeding, or purely random breeding, refined, not coarse hounds result. However, accepting dogs without the perfect balance is a necessity, not a virtue. The goal is the median, not somewhere on either side of it. Too many breeders and judges who should know better have accepted either refined "Deerhoundy" dogs without the requisite strength, or strong Mastiff- or Great Dane–like dogs without requisite speed or Greyhound-like form. Even those who do know better accept these off-type dogs. First, they do so unconsciously, or at least grudgingly. Later, they do so stealthily or defensively. Finally, they brazenly assert that one or the other represents correct type. When breeders not only produce but also *promote* either side of the median, and when judges sanction these hounds by awarding them prizes, they weaken the required vigilance to maintain type. Mastiffs reflect the premium placed on strength—enormous, broad, short-muzzled heads, large ears hanging close to the skull; thick necks and bodies; huge legs; wide, flat backs; and sharply angulated or rectangular overall shapes. Greyhounds display the goal of speed—compared to the Mastiff, narrower, longer heads with longer muzzles, little stop, and small rose ears; longer, less thick necks; longer legs; longer backs, arched-over loins; overall shape demonstrating ovals, soft curves, and the flowing lines that bespeak speed first, and then strength.

The Irish Wolfhound, although Greyhound-like in form, stands midway between the Mastiff and the Greyhound. Taller than the Mastiff but not so broad, thick, and angular and hence not so powerful as the Mastiff; Greyhound-like in form, but to quote the eighteenth-century Goldsmith, "more robust" and consequently not so swift as the Greyhound—this is the Irish Wolfhound. Combining power and speed once served a practical purpose—catching and dispatching wolves. Today, when we no longer hunt wolves with Irish Wolfhounds, balance lies at the essence of type. An Irish Wolfhound that lacks the requisite balance between speed and power deviates from proper type.

Ch. Roise of Ambleside, owned by Suzanne B. Rowe.   *Evelyn M. Shafer*

"... in General Type He Is a Rough-Coated Greyhoundlike Breed"

The dog with a perfect balance between power and speed and which has "great size and [a] commanding appearance" has a great deal. However, if great size, commanding appearance, and a perfect balance of power and speed be not found in a Greyhound-like *form* in an Irish Wolfhound, then to that extent that dog deviates from type. The Standard says "Greyhoundlike." Miss Susan Hudson (Brabyns Kennels, England), breeder and international judge, told me, "Breeders should never forget that the Irish Wolfhound is a member of the Greyhound family, not the Mastiff." The Greyhound the Standard's drafters had in mind was not the Greyhound bred for conformation showing that we see at all-breed dog shows. These tall, elegant, extreme, narrow, clumsy dogs are in complete opposition to the ideal of a "Greyhoundlike" Irish Wolfhound, as incidentally they also are to today's best strong, swift, working Greyhounds. The reproduction from Stonehenge's Greyhounds constitutes the type the drafters had in mind when they wrote our Standard.

The essence of the Greyhound-like requirement lies in two characteristics: length and soft curves. The late Miss Noreen Twyman (Nendrum Kennels, Ireland), in her genius for brevity, described the essence of soft curves at the judge's dinner following the 1978 IWCA Specialty. She said, "When you think of Irish Wolfhounds, think of ovals, not angles." She referred to the Greyhound's soft curves, not the Great Dane's harsh angles.

The history of the Irish Wolfhound is replete with references as a tall, massive Greyhound. Over and over, it appears. I have included a sample of these references, only to impress how fundamental the Greyhound form is to proper Irish Wolfhound type:

> 1770, Oliver Goldsmith: "He was made extremely like a Greyhound, but rather more robust."
>
> 1774, Smith: "Much taller than the Mastiff, but more like a Greyhound, and for size, strength, and shape, cannot be equalled."
>
> 1775, Twiss: "Much taller than a Mastiff, or any dog I had seen; they appeared to be of great strength, and their shape somewhat that of a Greyhound."
>
> 1790, Berwick: "The Irish Greyhound is the largest of the dog kind, and its appearance the most beautiful. These dogs are

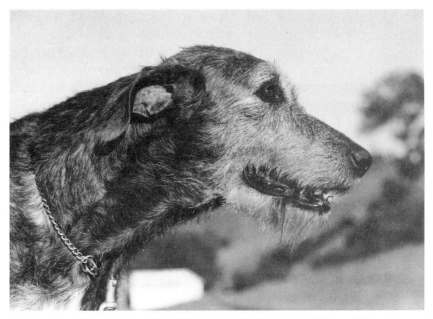

This head study illustrates a number of important points in the Irish Wolfhound Standard, most important of which is the unmistakable Greyhound-like type, which is so essential to the correct stamp.   *Joan Ludwig*

"Commanding appearance" even in repose is one of the most important essentials any Irish Wolfhound must possess.

about three feet high, somewhat like a Greyhound, but more robust. Their aspect is mild, their disposition peaceable, their strength so great that in combat the Mastiff or Bulldog is far from being equal to them. They mostly seize their antagonists by the back and shake them to death, which their great strength enables them to do."

1797, *Encyclopaedia Britannica:* "Very thick-set, tall Greyhound with rough coat, massive head."

1803, *Sportsman's Cabinet:* "Gigantic, rough Greyhound of great power."

1847, Nenis MacCarthy describing Mac Eoin's Greyhound:

> As fly the shadows o'er the grass
>   He flies with step as light and sure;
> He hunts the wolf in Trouston's Pass, . . .
> His stature tall, his body long,
>   His back like night, his breast like snow,
> His foreleg, pillar-like and strong,
>   His hindleg like a bended bow;
> Rough, curling hair, head long and thin,
>   His ear a leaf so small and round; . . .

1847, Lord Derby: "She was a dark brindle, heavier in build and more massive than a Deerhound, ears lying close to the head. She was very large, and very noble in appearance."

1859, *Gazetteer of the World:* "The Irish Greyhound is seldom met with, its appearance is beautiful and majestic, its height about three feet, its courage and strength so great that the Mastiff or Bulldog is far from equal to it."

THE SPECIAL PARTS OF THE STANDARD

Head and Neck

"Head—Long, the frontal bones of the forehead very slightly raised and very little indentation between the eyes. Skull, not too broad. Muzzle, long and moderately pointed."

The Standard devotes more words to the Irish Wolfhound's head than to any other part, including forequarters and hindquarters. Why this emphasis on the head? Because, except for the animal as a whole, nothing stamps type on the dog more than its head. "The head appears to be the first and most important point, inasmuch as it, more than anything else, is a proof of purity," wrote a successful mid-Victorian breeder and judge, whose words referred to Mastiffs but apply as well to Irish Wolfhounds. Furthermore, of all the parts of the dog, the head is most noticed. Forequarters, hindquarters, chest, back, and neck—all are critical, but it is the head that attracts the most attention most of the time, particularly when one is communicating with the dog.

The Irish Wolfhound has a Greyhound-shaped head with a gazehound expression. Captain Graham wrote that the proper head should be

> long, but not narrow, coming to a comparative point towards the nose; nose rather large, and head gradually getting broader from the same, *evenly* up to the back of the skull—not sharp up to the eyes, and then suddenly broad and lumpy, as is often the case with dogs bred between the Greyhound and Mastiff.

The Irish Wolfhound's head is long, with approximately as much length in front of the eyes as behind them, the skull is flat, there is little or no stop between skull and muzzle, and the head tapers, that is, comes to a *comparative* point at the nose. To distinguish it from both the Greyhound and the Deerhound, which it otherwise resembles, the Irish Wolfhound skull is *comparatively* broader, and the muzzle not so pointed. The Irish Wolfhound's head contrasts markedly with the Mastiff's head, which has a broad, round, or domed skull, and a short broad muzzle that ideally is nearly equal in width to the nose. Any of these characteristics seriously violate the Standard in the Irish Wolfhound. Breeders should always breed away from any hint of the Mastiff look in the head. Equally incorrect in the Irish Wolfhound, breeders should avoid the Great Dane head, with its finely chiseled look and prominent, full stop, and the full, square muzzle with a blunt, vertical front at the mouth. Hence, the requirement that the Irish Wolfhound head be Greyhound-*like*, resembling but not duplicating either the Greyhound or the Deerhound, and contrasting sharply with the broader, shorter, rounded head of the Mastiff, or the chiseled, rectangular, prominently stopped head of the Great Dane.

"Ears, small and Greyhoundlike in carriage."

The Irish Wolfhound's ears also resemble the Greyhound's and contrast with the Mastiff's and the Great Dane's. The Irish Wolfhound's ears, as the Greyhound's, are small, folded or rose, and carried back and close to the skull. The Mastiff's ears are large, and they hang flat. These qualities are an abomination in the Irish Wolfhound. The Great Dane's ears are not so large as the Mastiff's, but larger than the Irish Wolfhound's. When not subjected to cropping, they droop forward in contrast to the Irish Wolfhound's rose ears. Large, flat, pendulous, or drooping ears detract seriously from proper Irish Wolfhound type. Only the small, rose ear set fairly high on the skull, displays the Greyhound-like look the Irish Wolfhound Standard requires.

Captain Graham describes the proper Irish Wolfhound ears thus:

> Small in proportion to size of head, and half erect as in the smooth Greyhound. If dark in color it is to be preferred.

"Eyes, dark."

The eyes must have that characteristic, far-off gazehound look "that we have come to know and love in the Irish Wolfhound," as Mrs. Jenkins has said. Only dark, slightly almond-shaped, soft eyes can fully express the Irish Wolfhound type. Light eyes detract from the proper expression. Bold, staring, large eyes, however dark, can never properly reflect the soft, far-off gazehound expression, although occasionally such eyes mar otherwise beautiful heads.

Coat, "especially wiry and long over eyes and under jaw."

The Irish Wolfhound, like the Scottish Deerhound, should have ample face furnishings—especially the beard and the characteristic grizzled hair above the eyes that typify the highest-quality heads.

Mouth

The Standard makes no mention of the proper Irish Wolfhound mouth. This disturbs some people, particularly judges, a few of whom have almost a mouth fetish. We don't know why the original English Standard omitted a section on mouths. The drafters of the American Standard, who had the chance to add such a section, chose not to do so in the revision of 1950. One thing is clear, however: both the English and the American breeders recognized the importance of proper mouths. The two most important elements in correct mouths are: (1) correct jaw construction and (2) suitable teeth. Large, powerful jaws were essential when Irish Wolfhounds hunted wolves—to grab and to hold on to them once caught.

Today, of course, Irish Wolfhounds do not hunt wolves; indeed, most never hunt. Nevertheless, jaws should have the size and strength to do the job originally intended. Properly constructed mouths are neither undershot—the lower jaw protruding beyond the upper jaw—not overshot—the upper jaw protruding too far beyond the lower jaw. The proper construction, called bite, is an upper jaw that either protrudes slightly beyond the lower jaw (scissors bite) or is level with it (even bite). Too many novices and, surprisingly, judges confuse improperly set teeth with improper jaw construction. Many Irish Wolfhounds have one or two crooked upper or lower incisors. This trivial hereditary trait (curiously, they occur mainly in males) does not in the slightest interfere with the mouth's function and ought not to concern breeders or judges. For some reason, however, it occasionally generates heated, if totally useless, debate. Crooked incisors matter not a jot either in function or proper form of the Irish Wolfhound.

Size and number of teeth *do* matter. Irish Wolfhounds should have a *full* set of *full-sized* teeth. Surprisingly, many (and the numbers seem to be increasing) have small and even missing bicuspids and molars. If not actually dysfunctional in an age when Irish Wolfhounds eat prepared foods, the hereditary deterioration both in size and existence is not correct. Curiously, checking a dog's mouth to most judges means simply looking at bite. Except for a few English judges, in whose country, oddly enough, small and missing teeth rarely occur, I have not seen judges look for this growing phenomenon in Irish Wolfhounds in the American show ring.

One other point about mouths, which like the crooked incisors is largely aesthetic, is that Irish Wolfhounds' lips should be black. We are seeing too much pigment dilution or even its total absence. Breeders should breed away from the liver, or worse, pink lips we are beginning to see all too often, and judges should consider color in their assessment of mouths. Irish Wolfhound mouths, in summary, should include in order of importance: (1) large, powerful jaws that produce a scissors or even bite; (2) a full set of fully developed teeth; and (3) black pigment in the lips.

The Irish Wolfhound head overall, and in all its particulars, should resemble the Greyhound's head, except the Irish Wolfhound's head is *comparatively* heavier than the latter's. Anything that hints of Mastiff or Great Dane violates type, should be emphatically bred away from, and should be heavily penalized in competition. Hence, look for *comparatively* long, tapered heads; little or no stop; small, rose ears; soft, dark eyes with that far-off gazehound look; and the grizzled, bearded furnishings to finish a quality head. Avoid coarse, thick, rounded, short, and chiseled heads; heads bare of furnishings; large, flat, pendulous ears; and bold or staring expressions. Leave all these latter characteristics to Mastiffs and Great Danes, where some, or all, properly belong.

"Neck—Rather long, very strong and muscular, well arched, without dewlap or loose skin about the throat."

Irish Wolfhound necks, like typical Irish Wolfhounds in general, are strong and graceful. Muscular necks, the Standard calls for in order to give the hounds strength. Well-arched necks give not only the impression of strength but also of quality and beauty. Clean necks also reflect quality and beauty. Loose, hanging skin under the neck in the form of a dewlap both detracts from the Greyhound-like form and suggests clumsiness. All agree that necks should be arched, muscular, and clean.

About length of neck, controversy arises. There are those who believe that the longer the neck the more correct the dog. This is not true. Admittedly, the hound whose head seems to come straight out of its shoulders is not only displeasing but also cannot "gaze" for its quarry or house the Greyhound-like form. However, the long, giraffe-like necks we are seeing all too often are also incorrect. Notice that the Standard does not say long necks, but qualifies the requirement. It reads: "rather long." More striking, Captain Graham did not mention length in describing the proper Irish Wolfhound neck. He wrote, "Necks should be thick in comparison to its form, and very muscular." Since he was so careful to state his views, it is not likely that he would inadvertently omit to mention length of neck. He must have considered strength most important in correct necks. Of course, in a breed where length is important overall, it would destroy symmetry to have a short neck. Hence, the Standard's "rather long" ingeniously captures the concept of balance—a neck

Necks

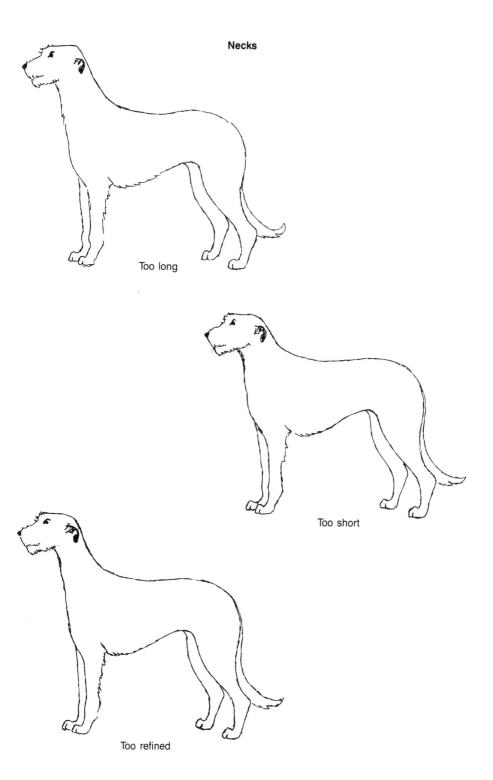

Too long

Too short

Too refined

long enough to comport with a gazehound's form, but strong enough to enable the hound to dispatch a wolf.

Years ago, when I *thought* I had learned something about necks, I had the effrontery to tell Mrs. Nagle that I thought Irish Wolfhound necks should be as long as possible. Using one of her characteristically forthright expressions, she called me "a stupid idiot" and followed up her blunt comment with a letter in which the following enlightening words appeared:

> I thought I had learnt the hard way not to speak my mind to Americans, but I thought you were a stupid idiot [in what you said about necks]. . . . A Wolfhound is not a Greyhound that has to reach down to get a hare, but needs a strong powerful neck to pull a wolf down. . . . [As to calling you a] "stupid idiot," how do you suppose I have earned my nickname Flick or Flicker if I did not have the reputation of flicking everybody on the raw. I try to be objective and see things as they are and not what one wants them to be. . . .

I was suitably "flicked." Whenever I judge Irish Wolfhounds, or whenever the subject of length of neck arises, I remember these words from this wise, plain-spoken expert on our breed and its Standard.

Neck set—that is, how the neck fits into the body—is critical to correct Irish Wolfhound conformation. The neck must set into the body at an angle that allows for gazehound function—to hold the head high to survey a territory, spot quarry, and keep prey in view until close enough to utilize scent. Gazehounds hold their heads high before galloping, and from time to time to survey a territory. They never—or should never—hold their heads high when galloping, and will lower their heads in movement depending both on speed and the necessity for using scent as opposed to sight. Hence, a neck set too low on the body, which we used to see frequently, does not allow for the high head carriage needed for the gazehound look. On the other extreme, a neck set too high, resulting in a ewe neck, does not permit the lowered head needed for efficient galloping and the effective use of scent.

Other faults accompany the ewe neck, the latter an increasingly prevalent fault that seems to have replaced the neck "stuck on the front of the body" we used to see so much in the 1960s and 1970s. Frequently, long, weak, thin, "giraffe-like" necks go hand in hand with ewe necks. These ugly, totally unacceptable necks look almost like tubes—no muscle and no shape—and nearly always signal an

Necks

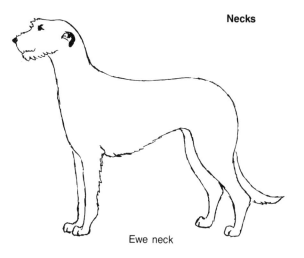

Ewe neck

Poorly set

"Stuck-on"

incorrect total front assembly. (See Forequarters below.) Either in combination or alone, the ewe and giraffe-like necks fundamentally violate the Standard. Breeders must breed away from them; judges must regard them as serious flaws that contradict the Standard's command regarding essential type—that the Irish Wolfhound combine power and speed in a Greyhound-like shape.

Finally, the neck must not only sit on the body at the proper angle, but it must also "flow" smoothly into the body in a gentle unbroken curve, from its arch at the base of the skull, through the shoulders. The neck set contributes to the magnificent long, unbroken, flowing line from the arch at the base of the skull, through the shoulders along the back, rising slightly over the loin, eventually ending at the tip of the gently upward sweep of the tail seen in the highest quality, typical hounds. Of course, more than the neck itself contributes to the neck set, particularly the shoulder construction and placement. Bad shoulders almost always accompany ewe necks. The proper neck set and resulting soft, curving, flowing, proper neckline pleases all who see it; the abrupt, almost right-angled, sharp, ugly line that characterizes the ewe neck jars the eye offensively. Leave these necks to sheep, and the tube necks to giraffes, who can use them, and hence whose conformation they fit so well.

Forequarters

Great size and commanding appearance, combining power and speed in a Greyhound-like form depends to a great extent on the proper forequarters. The forequarters include (1) shoulders, (2) forechest, (3) front legs, and (4) feet.

"Shoulders, muscular, giving breadth of chest, set sloping."

The well-laid shoulder contributes to the correct Greyhound-like form. It is also essential to proper movement. Along with the correct back and hindquarters, the shoulder makes it possible to trot easily and gallop effectively. The better laid the shoulder, the more likely the dog will have adequate extension or reach. The greater the reach, the longer the stride, assuming proper rear and back construction. Furthermore, the well-laid shoulder prevents pounding, or inefficient, uncomfortable movement. (See Chapter 10, "Wolfhound Gait," for full details.)

146

Shoulders

Correct

Stuck-on front

Upright

The correct Irish Wolfhound shoulder has three requirements: (1) it is laid-back, or angulated; (2) it is set sloping inward toward the withers; and (3) the *tip* of the shoulder blade is in a straight line with the elbow. The correct Irish Wolfhound shoulder pleases both the eye and the hand. It looks smooth, contributes to the smooth, correct neckline, and it feels smooth to the touch. "Lean" describes the shoulder, not "weak." No great bunches of muscles, or lumps, but a smooth touch to the hand. The withers, or tips of the shoulder blades, are gently sloped toward each other, increasingly so as the dog lowers its head to move.

An English breeder told me, "No more than three fingers between the withers at attention, Mr. Samaha." She meant, you cannot fit more than three fingers between the tips of the shoulder blades when the dog is standing with its head *up*. (Withers will always come close together when the dog lowers its head.) I took her literally, and for months after that, I put my fingers between the shoulder blades of every Irish Wolfhound I could, happy to apply my newly discovered formula for determining correct Irish Wolfhound shoulders. Like all simple formulas, of course, it was too simple. You cannot determine properly sloped shoulders so mechanistically.

Nevertheless, the general point stands: withers should not be spread wide apart in the stationary dog, and three or four fingers' width is not a bad estimate. Not only are correct shoulders sloped and the distance between them narrow, but the withers are also considerably narrower than the hips. Another experienced breeder told me, when I was starting out, to stand behind the dog and look forward. The general shape should be triangular—the hips forming the base of the triangle and the withers the tip. I still use this when judging dogs. After I finish going over the parts, I always stand squarely behind the dog and look forward toward the shoulder. Most Irish Wolfhounds fail the "triangle" test.

Straight, or upright, shoulders depart from the proper Greyhound-like form and make movement restricted and uncomfortable. Therefore breeders should breed away from them, and judges should penalize them. Shoulders that do not slope toward the withers frequently accompany upright shoulders, but not always. Shoulders without proper slope also depart from type. A serious problem pervades the Irish Wolfhound at the present time—the increasing number of upright shoulders set on without slope, wedded to either the long giraffe neck or the ewe neck. These unholy marriages are producing progeny that breeders during the 1990s may find difficult to control and correct.

Upper Arm—"Elbows well under, neither turned inwards nor outwards."

The correct Irish Wolfhound shoulder should, but frequently does not, connect to a comparatively long upper arm of the same angle as the properly laid shoulder. Nearly all Irish Wolfhounds today have both short and straight upper arms. Short, straight upper arms spoil type, not to mention their being unsightly. Moreover, they impede proper movement because without an upper arm with adequate length set at a comparable angle to the shoulder, the dog lacks the natural cushion such angles provide. Finally, the short, straight upper arm restricts the dog's reach, hence producing a short stride. The short, straight upper arm, always a problem in Irish Wolfhounds, appears at this writing so stamped into the breed's heredity that it is unlikely that we will see its reduction, let alone its demise, for some time to come. The dogs and bitches simply do not exist from which to breed in this critical element in the front assembly of the Irish Wolfhound.

"Forearm muscular, and the whole leg strong and quite straight."

Correct forelegs are long, straight, and strong. "Plenty of room underneath," said the best old breeders. Long legs bespeak not only long stride but also the Greyhound-like look. Dogs with short legs, or too close to the ground, can never signify the Greyhound-like form. No galloping animal has short legs; the correct Irish Wolfhound cannot have them either.

Long legs are necessary to proper conformation, but they are not sufficient to constitute correct forelegs in the Irish Wolfhound. Straight they must also be; not twisted or bent, as they too often are even in otherwise powerful hounds of high quality and correct form. The elbows should be set well under the body, not loosely extending out from it.

Moreover, the forelegs must be strong, meaning they possess plenty of bone and muscle. Poor hounds frequently lack bone in the foreleg. Captain Graham quoted with approval this description of the correct Irish Wolfhound foreleg:

The bone of the fore-leg is, I should say, the point that best distinguishes dogs of this class from all of the Greyhound class, whom in actual build they so much resemble. The massiveness of that bone is out of proportion altogether, and it certainly was not made for speed so much as for power and endurance. I think all the Scotch dogs [Scottish Deerhounds] that I have seen are deficient in this respect, and I attribute it to crossing with lighter-built breeds in order to obtain swiftness for deer-hunting.

Hounds with sufficient bone can, and all too often do, lack adequate muscle in the front leg. Breeders and judges must pay attention to *both* bone and muscle in the foreleg. Of course, adequate bone with inadequate muscle is preferable to inadequate bone *and* muscle, or adequate muscle without adequate bone. However, the forelegs with the best shape are long, straight, and derive their strength from both sufficient bone and muscle.

The pasterns, or the forelegs from the knee to the foot, should be slightly bent to give flexibility without weakness. Overbent pasterns (the dog is said to be "down in the pasterns") create weakness, while dogs with wholly straight pasterns, or worse, that are "knuckled over," rarely move properly and emanate discomfort. It is almost painful even to look at these dogs, which, it seems, are on the verge of tipping right over. I have seen dogs down in their pasterns move well, although they virtually always flap their feet around, sometimes in the most unsightly manner. The best-moving Irish Wolfhound I ever owned was badly down in his pasterns and flapped his front feet all over the place, despite Rachel Page Elliot's insistence that no dog with weak pasterns could move well. On the other hand, I have never seen a knuckled-over Irish Wolfhound move well.

"Feet—Moderately large and round, neither turned inwards nor outwards. Toes, well arched and closed. Nails, very strong and curved."

Irish Wolfhounds should have large, strong feet with thick nails and pads. The flat (as opposed to the correct "well arched and closed" toes) are both ugly and dysfunctional. These weak feet are noticeable at first sight. Not so obvious but equally important, thin pads with delicate nails also violate the Standard. The phrase "moderately large and round" is ambiguous with respect to "round." Does it mean moderately round, or simply round? Some maintain that "round" is correct, that "moderately" modifies "large." Others

Pasterns

Knuckled over

Correct

Sloping

Forechest

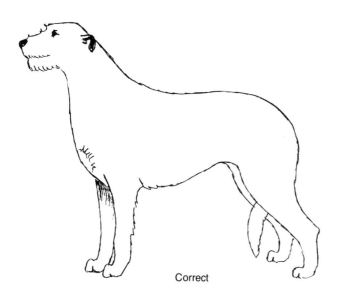

Correct

Insufficient

152

maintain that "moderately round" refers to the hare foot, or one with the two middle toes extending significantly out from the outer two, quite in contrast to the perfectly round cat feet.

Irish Wolfhounds, according to the Standard, should turn their feet neither "inwards nor outwards." The "pigeon-toed" Irish Wolfhound, or one whose feet turn inward, clearly has improper feet. As their name suggests, they belong on pigeons, not on Irish Wolfhounds. The pigeon-toed Irish Wolfhound will almost certainly "toe-in" and put weight on the outside of the foot when it moves, signaling both inefficient and unsightly movement. The Irish Wolfhound that stands with feet perfectly straight will almost surely toe-in slightly when moving. Only those that stand with feet turned *slightly* out will bring their feet into the center of gravity and put their weight squarely onto the pads in a straight position while trotting. (See Chapter 10, "Wolfhound Gait.")

The Greyhound expert quoted in Stonehenge makes this revealing comment about feet, which he regarded as a "minor point" in assessing proper type:

> With regard to . . . well-formed feet much difference of opinion has arisen, and most courses advocate the selection of the catlike foot . . . ; but I do not myself care for more than a moderately short one, provided the knuckles are powerful and well-up, and that the toes do not spread; and provided also that the sole is thick, and covered with a good horny skin.

This comment probably summarizes best the elements of, and the controversy surrounding, a minor point, rated eleventh in order of merit, in the Standard.

"Chest—Very deep. Breast, wide."

The body of the Irish Wolfhound includes the chest, the back, and the croup. Captain Graham said,

> The body should give an impression of nice length rather than the idea of a short-coupled-up body.

According to the Standard, the correct chest is "very deep," and the breast "wide." Notice that the chest should be "very" deep, but the breast only "wide." Miss Elizabeth Murphy, Carrokeel Kennels, Ireland, in the excellent discussion of type in her book *The Irish Wolfhound,* correctly describes the proper chest:

Fronts

Correct Front

Typical puppy front

Fronts

Toeing out

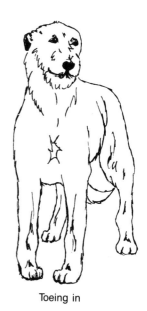

Toeing in

Tied at elbows

Too narrow, fine bone

Too wide, heavy bone

155

> Viewed from the front, the well-sprung rib cage would appear egg-shaped with the wider part at the top.

In other words, the chest should be deeper than it is wide. Correct chests rule out both the barrel-chested and the slab-sided dog.

Captain Graham said that "the ribs [should be] reasonably sprung, but not . . . so as to resemble a barrel-like appearance."

Too many breeders are prejudiced on this point. Those who saw too many thick-set, short-coupled dogs during the period when type was badly deteriorating, viewed dogs with proper spring of rib as barrel-chested. Those who saw too many long, flat-backed, narrow, refined hounds, were calling dogs with proper spring of rib "slab-sided." If all keep in mind Miss Murphy's perfect definition—"egg-shaped"—they will have little trouble identifying the correct Irish Wolfhound chest.

The brisket, or breast, meaning the combined bone and muscle extending back from between the forelegs, should run parallel to the ground for a considerable distance. We see far too many hounds with two serious faults in the brisket: (1) they are too narrow-breasted; and (2) their briskets are too short, that is, they do not run back long enough from the forelegs. Captain Graham said the "brisket [should be] down to the elbows and nicely wide at the bottom."

The narrow-breasted hounds nearly always lack both forechest and width across the chest. Narrow-breasted dogs fit Mrs. Nagle's description of the dog that looks like "both its front legs are coming out of the same hole." These hounds nearly always are too narrow all the way through, that is, they have narrow heads, weak, thin necks, refined legs, slab sides, and narrow hips. They are, in Mrs. Nagle's matchless phrases, the "steamroller dogs," or "silhouettes beautiful in outline but that you can't see them coming or going," which she appropriately labeled "abominations."

The Irish Wolfhound's brisket should run parallel to the ground for a sufficient distance back from the forelegs. Precisely how long is correct? Miss Murphy says that the brisket should run two-thirds the length of the rib cage. I cannot reduce it to so precise a fraction, but I am certain that "herring guts," those unsightly under-lines that turn abruptly upward shortly beyond the foreleg, belong on the fish after which they were named. The correct Irish Wolf-hound underline, as all other parts, requires soft, curving lines, not abrupt angles.

Stonehenge's Greyhound expert, as in so many instances, put

Underlines

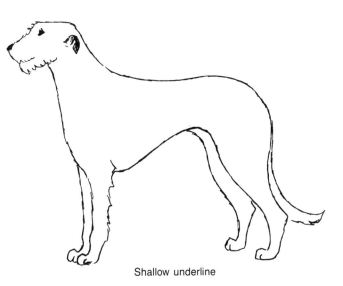

Shallow underline

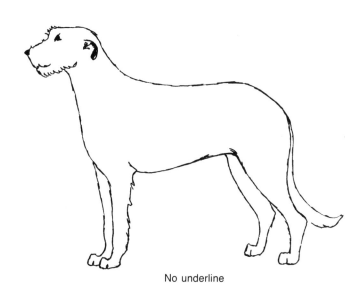

No underline

the case for the egg-shaped chest that balances depth and breadth in words no one has improved for the Irish Wolfhound:

> With regard to the *chest,* there are two things to be considered— namely, capacity for the lodgment of the lungs and heart, and the attainment of that form most conducive to speed and working. It must not be too deep, or the animal is constantly striking it against obstacles; it must not be too wide, or the shoulders are unable to play smoothly upon it, as they must do in the action of this quarter; but it must be of sufficient capacity to lodge the heart and lungs. A just relation between these three counterbalancing essentials is therefore the best form—neither too small for good wind, nor too wide for speed, nor too deep to keep free from the irregularities of the ground, but that happy medium which we see in our best specimens, and which the portraits of most of our best dogs will exhibit to the eye of the courser.

"Belly—Well drawn up."

To finish the underline, Irish Wolfhounds should have bellies well tucked up, but not extremely so. Dogs with an underline running nearly parallel to the ground, which we see more frequently in dogs than bitches for some reason I do not understand, cannot possibly conform to the Greyhound-like shape. A dog at the other extreme whose belly is tucked up so as to be "wasp-waisted" is equally wrong. Far too many judges and breeders believe that the more tuck-up the better. But as in everything regarding the Irish Wolfhound, moderation, not extremes, rules the Standard. The wasp waist is ugly, and suggests and often reflects weak backs in particular and refined structure in general. We do not want, and the Standard forbids, Irish Wolfhounds that resemble wasps in any way.

"Back—Rather long than short. Loins, arched."

This part of the Standard has occasioned enormous controversy, particularly the phrase "rather long than short." Does it mean the longer the better? Sort of long? How long is long? Of course, Irish Wolfhounds must have backs long enough to comport with the general requirement of length discussed in the General Appearance section. Furthermore, this requirement of length not only specifies the Greyhound-like look, but it also serves the functional aim of a galloping hound that can cover ground.

Toplines

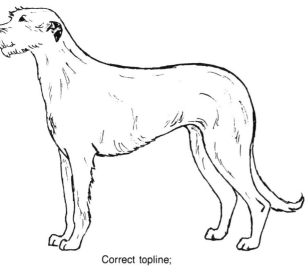

Correct topline;
neckline, and underline

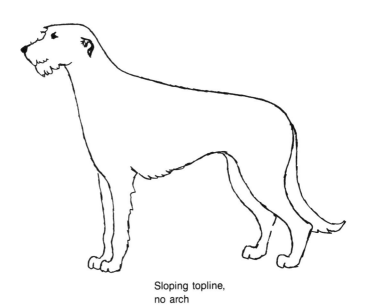

Sloping topline,
no arch

Toplines

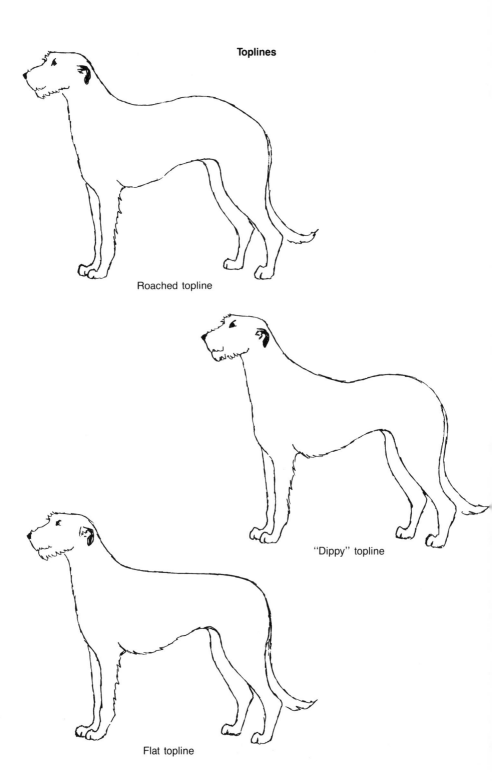

Roached topline

"Dippy" topline

Flat topline

Every inch in length of back results in an inch greater stride, simply by construction. However, this does not mean that the longer the back the better. A critical point to remember: length of stride is purchased eventually at the price of strength, symmetry, and balance. Stonehenge made this point:

> It must be self-evident that every inch in length of back increases the stride by that amount exactly, and therefore if prolonged indefinitely it would be advantageous, till counterbalanced by the disadvantages inseparably connected with this form, in consequence of the diminished strength.

He goes on to point out something that we often ignore—the difference in the entire length from the neck and forechest, as opposed to the length of the loin specifically. It is too much length in the loin that causes the weakness, not the length from the forechest to the end of the rib cage. Length of rib cage and breast adds strength; proper length of loin adds to strength and ability to gallop. Having too long a loin produces weakness:

> The length of back should therefore be looked for between the neck and the last rib, rather than between the last rib and the hip bone; and this is a very important consideration too often neglected.

In addition to the weakness and imbalance it generates, the excessively long loin virtually always accompanies two intolerable faults in the topline—the flat and slack backs. These ugly toplines, the flat back even more than the slack back, violate the essential Greyhound-like flowing curves from neck to tail. These aberrations in type and function often appear attractive to those ignorant of proper Irish Wolfhound conformation. These long, flat backs crop up periodically as fads that novices, ignorant judges, and even too many breeders cave in to. Apparently, this is nothing new.

Stonehenge refers to the flat-back vogue during the nineteenth century in this revealing quote:

> It was the fashion from 1840 to 1850 to select flat and straight backs, and these certainly are handsomer than the high-arched backs previously so much in vogue. . . . [P]ossibly partly in consequence of the attention which I drew to this point, the very level back is not so much in fashion, and the arched loin . . . is much sought after.

According to Captain Graham,

> the loin should be a little full, but not so exaggerated as to give the hound the appearance of being dipped behind the shoulder, but just

sufficient to give a nice gradual sweep right down to the set-on of the tail, which should connect fairly low down. This all adds to the lines of a nice set of curves beginning with the crest of the neck and finishing with the bend of the tail.

Mrs. Nagle recognized the trend toward flat backs, and their wide popularity among those not schooled in the history of the breed and uneducated in type generally. In addition to narrow dogs in general, few characteristics disturbed her more than Irish Wolfhounds whose loins were too long and flat. She particularly feared them because they appealed aesthetically to the uneducated Irish Wolfhound breeders that cropped up in such great numbers during the 1960s and 1970s.

This fear of the long, flat loin led some breeders to go to the other extreme, breeding for short-coupled dogs. These dogs not only violate the specific call for general length, but they also lack balance and symmetry. Furthermore, like the narrow dogs, the short-coupled dogs seem always to possess their own related faults—barrel chests, wheel backs, or any variety of over-arched loins, steep croups, and straight stifles. These faults do not always appear together, but they seem to do so much of the time. Why these faults marry each other I cannot say, but they are faults as serious as the cluster of faults surrounding the narrow dogs. Breeders should breed away from both extremes, and judges should search for and reward the medium in the show ring whenever possible.

Hindquarters

"Hindquarters—Muscular thighs and second thighs long and strong as in the Greyhound, and hocks well let down and turning neither in nor out."

Captain Graham said,

The hindquarters are responsible for about two-thirds of his movement, continued movement that is, given the hound is fit internally. He needs good, strong hindquarters, well muscled up, as separated from the superabundance of fat. . . .

The hindquarters are, in Mrs. Nagle's felicitous phrase, "the engine that drives the Irish Wolfhound." She went even further than Captain Graham, contending not only that they contributed to two-

Croup

Correct croup

Flat croup

Steep croup

thirds of the movement, but also that they are the most important single part of the dog. She often told me that you can breed good heads in a generation, but not the complex anatomy of the proper hindquarters. In order to emphasize this point, she established the Sulhamstead Trophy at the Irish Wolfhound Club of America's Specialty for the hound with the best hindquarters.

Many will disagree with her emphasis on the hindquarters, and to be sure these days the forequarters are in much worse shape. In fact, nothing throws my judging off more than to line the dogs up facing me—a nightmare even in collections of otherwise high-quality hounds. The view from the rear is much better, thanks in part to Mrs. Nagle's tireless efforts to breed for, and get others to concentrate on, the hindquarters. The hindquarters comprise five main parts: (1) the croup, (2) the thighs—from the hips to the stifles, (3) the second thighs and stifles, (4) the hocks, and (5) the feet.

Croup

The croup—the area from the end of the loin to the base of the tail—should slope gently into the tail. Flat croups do not slope enough, and often make more of an angle from loin to tail base than a curving line. Steep croups, or those that fall almost at a right angle off the loin into the base of the tail impair the flowing soft topline, and sometimes they interfere with proper movement. Dogs with steep croups sometimes do not have sufficient thrust or drive to accomplish the necessary length of stride either during trotting or galloping.

The correct croup not only slopes gently to the base of the tail, but it also has great width. It forms the base of the triangle that I mentioned in relation to the withers. Dogs with narrow croups not only exhibit weakness, but cannot meet the requirements of powerful hindquarters the Standard mandates.

Thighs

The correct Irish Wolfhound thighs have both length and strength. The thighs have the greatest muscle mass in the entire dog, even greater than the neck muscles, which are also powerful and thick. The thighs contribute to the great powerful thrusting drive that all the best Irish Wolfhounds have, in common with the coursing and racing Greyhounds. Thighs should not only be thick but

Stifles

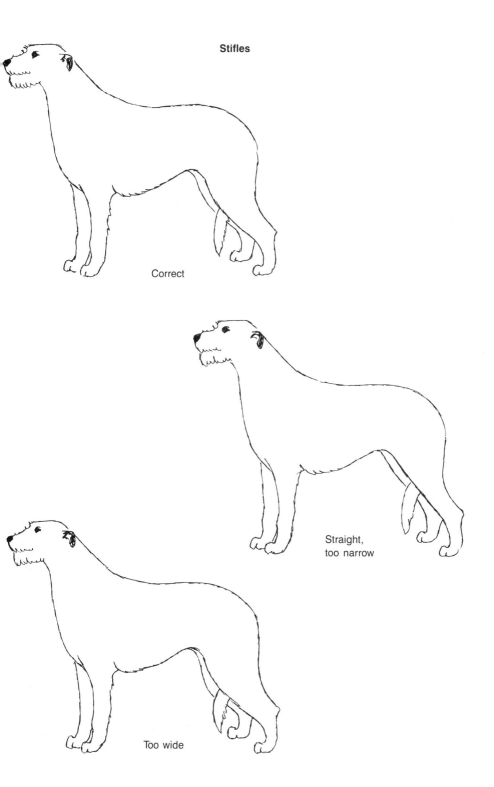

Correct

Straight,
too narrow

Too wide

wide; the unsightly narrow thighs suggest weakness, although I have seen many Irish Wolfhounds with power despite narrow thighs.

Second Thighs and Stifles

Captain Graham remarked that the Irish Wolfhound should have "nicely bent second thighs and stifles." Perhaps the most prevalent fault in the hindquarters that destroys the Greyhound-like look are straight, short stifles. The long, sweeping, nicely bent stifle both suggests the ability to take advantage of the thrust that powerful haunches and thighs provide and is essential to the general requirement of curves and the absence of lines and angles, seen in the best hounds. Furthermore, the straight, short stifle belongs in a draft animal, not a galloping dog—in a Mastiff, not an Irish Wolfhound.

Curiously, some straight, short-stifled dogs can move beautifully. I have seen these dogs, whose straight, abrupt, short lines when stationary turn into the desired splendid soft curves in motion. I have also seen dogs with long, sweeping stifles that somehow motion transforms into abrupt, unattractive, untypical angles and lines. I do not know why this should be so. However, the best-moving Irish Wolfhound I owned had straight shoulders, a short upper arm, a short wheel-back, a steep croup, and short, thick, straight stifles. In motion, he was all curves and fit perfectly the Standard's requirement that the Irish Wolfhound have "easy and active" movement. The best Irish Wolfhounds, of course, have balanced, symmetrical, soft curve when they are stationary *and* when in motion.

A prominent fault is lack of muscle in the second thigh. Without sufficient muscle in the second thigh, Irish Wolfhounds are not only weak, but they also do not look like Greyhounds. I have known people used to looking at dogs who are narrow all the way through the hindquarters—narrow hips, no muscle mass either in the thigh or second thigh—who ask when they see properly constructed hindquarters, "What are all these lumps?" These "lumps," I once heard Mrs. Nagle say with mixed consternation and humor, "are what I want to see on all my dogs, thank you very much." When she walked away, the puzzled questioner wondered what on earth she was talking about. All I could say is what I advise anyone who wants to know what proper Irish Wolfhound thighs and second thighs should look like: look at a coursing Greyhound from the rear. Those "lumps" you see are the musculature required to thrust and drive in the gallop.

Hocks

Correct

Too high

Too low

"Hocks well let down and turning neither in nor out."

The cow hock is the fault that novices learn first, and remember longest. The correct hock turns "neither in nor out." Equally important, sometimes never learned, and too often overlooked, is that hocks should be "well let down." High hocks are not a prevalent fault in the Irish Wolfhound but when they appear, impair the Greyhound-like look.

"Tail—Long and slightly curved, of moderate thickness, and well covered with hair."

The tail is the Irish Wolfhound's rudder, helping the hound take turns and retain balance while galloping. The tail reveals the Irish Wolfhound's emotions—up when excited, wagging of course when happy, tucked between its legs when afraid, up and bristling when provoked. The tail set and the tail carriage contribute to good conformation. The tail set on high wrecks the gazehound look, making Irish Wolfhounds look more like sporting dogs than galloping hounds. What is worse, the high-set tail almost often accompanies other intolerable faults—the flat back, the flat croup, and the "gay" tail, a tail carried high whenever the dog moves.

The short, thin tail—the "rat tail"—also violates the Standard. Anyone who has witnessed this fault knows well why the drafters called for a *long* tail. Anyone who has seen shortness married to thinness knows why the Standard calls for a moderately thick tail. Anyone who has seen a short, thin, gay tail knows how this deadly combination can wreck an otherwise beautiful hound. These tails destroy both balance and symmetry, detract seriously from proper conformation, and unequivocally demonstrate why gay "rat" tails should remain on happy rodents, not Irish Wolfhounds.

Coat

"Rough and hard on body, legs and head; especially wiry and long over eyes and under jaw."

In the nineteenth century, a heated debate arose over whether the Irish Wolfhound was originally a smooth-coated dog like the Greyhound or was wiry as we demand in our Standard. Captain Graham insisted that the Irish Wolfhound was a rough-coated dog,

Rears

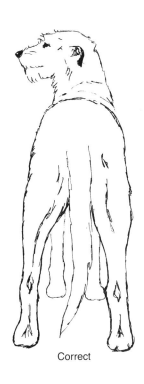

Correct

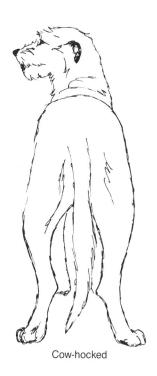

Cow-hocked

Narrow

not smooth. In fact, he criticized the Reinagle hound mainly because of its short coat. An otherwise good hound cannot meet the Standard without the typical rough coat seen on the best dogs. Long coats are as wrong as smooth coats; soft coats are also incorrect.

The proper Irish Wolfhound coat is truly harsh, grizzled, and of medium length. The long, harsh coats, although they do not satisfy the Standard fully, are to be preferred to the long, soft coats. When I judge, I do not penalize as much the smooth-coated Irish Wolfhounds that look too much like Greyhounds as I do the long, soft-coated hounds that resemble the sporting hounds. After all, Irish Wolfhounds that resemble Greyhounds too much do not satisfy the Standard fully, but Irish Wolfhounds that look like sporting dogs ought not to be in the gazehound group at all. In any event, the harsh, medium coat with especially prominent beard and eyebrow furnishings adds quality to any Irish Wolfhound—to the inexperienced and ignorant judges these typical coats may often hide serious faults in conformation.

Movement

"Easy and active."

In Chapter 10, McDowell Lyon provides a description of the basic movement in the Irish Wolfhound which I felt I could not improve upon. My own comments concerning movement appear in the Guide to Following the Judging of Irish Wolfhounds in Chapter 9.

"When I judge Irish Wolfhounds," Mrs. Nagle used to say, "I ask myself, which one of these dogs would I want by my side if I encountered a hungry wolf in wild country?" The goal, from Goldsmith in the eighteenth century to Captain Graham in the nineteenth to breeders of the Golden Age in America and on from them to the few stalwarts who carried on their legacy to us, and which we must strive to leave for those who follow us, is to preserve the precarious balance of type in the Irish Wolfhound—a beautiful dog of "great size and commanding appearance, remarkable for combining power and speed" in a *Greyhound-like* form.

A beautiful rear on a six-week-old puppy.

A happy three-month-old high-quality dog puppy.

An outstanding front assembly, from forechest to feet, in a three-month-old dog puppy.

7

The Irish Wolfhound Puppy

THIS CHAPTER is directed to novices, hopefully giving them some basic advice about selecting a puppy, when and how to get it, and how to introduce it to its new home. The Irish Wolfhound pushes nature to the extreme. Born weighing little more than a pound, not much more than the average-sized breed of dog, at six months the Irish Wolfhound puppy weighs one hundred pounds. One hundred pounds in half a year; the growth is akin to cancerous. Pushing nature carries risks. Much can go wrong, and often does in growing puppies. Remember that in choosing any puppy, you are buying a risk; Irish Wolfhound puppies exaggerate that risk. Of course, breeders frequently do, and should, assure new owners that the puppy they bought is free of parasites and other obvious health problems. Beyond that assurance, however, beware the seller who tells you that you have bought a "show" puppy, or a puppy "guaranteed" not to have genetic health problems. Anyone who tells you that either knows nothing about Irish Wolfhounds—or any living, growing thing for that matter—or is trying to hoodwink you.

GROUND RULES

Some reputable breeders do assume health, temperament, and conformation risks that may befall the Irish Wolfhound puppy. In fact, there are no *standard* arrangements that breeders make with those to whom they sell their stock. Only the imagination limits the specific arrangements. I have heard of breeders who will replace any puppy, anytime, that does not fulfill its potential, however they define potential. I have heard of money-back guarantees. I have heard of paying a small amount at weaning time; if at eighteen months, the puppy turns out healthy and of "show quality," then the buyer pays the remaining amount. Most frequently, responsible breeders inform buyers that they are purchasing potential and risk. This does not mean "as is" as in common merchandising—at least responsible breeders would never offer an Irish Wolfhound puppy for sale as if it were simply a piece of merchandise. It means that owners acquire puppies that are free from parasites and known diseases, that the breeders have given puppies the best care they know how from the time they bred their bitch to the time they sold the puppies.

When buying a puppy, then, the rank novice should choose a responsible breeder, not a specific puppy. To choose a breeder, contact the Irish Wolfhound Club of America. The Club regularly places ads in *Dog World, The Irish Wolfhound Quarterly,* and other publications. If you cannot find these, write to the American Kennel Club, 51 Madison Avenue, New York, NY 10010 for the name and address of the current IWCA secretary. The IWCA keeps a current list of breeders and owners in every region of the United States. The people on this list want to teach you about Irish Wolfhounds. They fully understand that satisfied owners mean happy Irish Wolfhounds. Most of these people will not have puppies to sell you immediately. Even if they do, they will not offer you one right away. Do not let this discourage you. Furthermore, realize that breeders do not "screen" you for reasons of social snobbery. They simply want to make sure that you really want an Irish Wolfhound.

☆　☆　☆

Two hours old—resting up from a hard journey through the birth canal.

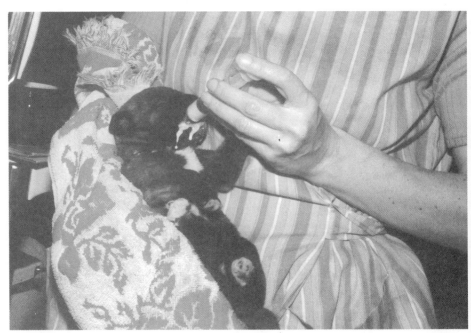

Ch. Meadowbrook Lust (Witchesbroom Maffiossi ex Meadowbrook Gwyn) at one week, hand-fed, as were her nine littermates. Her dam's milk mysteriously dried up.

NEWSPAPER ADS, RETAIL OUTLETS, AND REPUTABLE BREEDERS

Before turning to how to go about dealing with reputable breeders, let me say a few words about buying puppies from newspaper and magazine advertisements, or from commercial establishments selling Irish Wolfhounds. Since buying puppies is always a risk, and one which reputable breeders cannot accurately predict, why *not* buy a puppy from a newspaper advertisement, or a retail outlet if there is one nearby? Several reasons: First, most people who advertise in newspapers or who sell puppies commercially don't know anything about Irish Wolfhounds. Second, profit does not drive reputable breeders; they give *all* their puppies, whether pets or potential show and breeding stock, the best care they know how to provide. Third, they love their puppies, play with them, socialize them, and generally treat them as special living things, not as pieces of merchandise. Fourth, reputable breeders, who give so much of themselves, experience such disappointment, heartache, and expense, deserve the support of all those who love our breed. Fifth, reputable breeders do not regularly charge more than others for their puppies. Prices vary so widely that I cannot quote an average price; if I could, it would not mean anything. Two breeders in the same area, or the same breeder with different litters, may charge different prices. However, clearly you cannot assume that it will be "cheaper" and will not be "better" buying from ads and retail stores. Finally, we need to do all we can to discourage indiscriminate breeding of Irish Wolfhounds, the surest road to dilution and disintegration of type and quality. We never want to face again the crisis brought on by the population explosion of the 1970s.

In the long run, you and Irish Wolfhounds will benefit from the time you spend with both the reputable breeders you contact and with their hounds, *before* you buy a puppy. Go to as many of these people as you can. Spend time with their dogs at home, so you know what it's like having an Irish Wolfhound. People who admire them from a distance often change their minds when they face them—literally. Know what it is like to have an Irish Wolfhound at eye level, breathing on you, leaning on you, commonly nudging you as you sit in a chair. Experience the odor that emanates from a large dog, no matter how clean. Experience an Irish Wolfhound's appearance in the living room after dinner with the remains of a beef roast

A five-week-old dog puppy resting in order to grow.

A five-week-old bitch puppy—they don't *always* sleep.

clenched happily between its jaws. Watch an adult Irish Wolfhound urinate and defecate to see just how much it can produce. On a walk, have an Irish Wolfhound pull you effortlessly to the ground by the leash when it spies something it wants to investigate further. Mrs. Nagle exposed me to all these experiences numerous times before she agreed to sell me Sulhamstead Felix, the ancestor to all the Meadowbrook hounds. When I got him, I *knew* I wanted an Irish Wolfhound.

SELECTING A BREEDER

Suppose, after these visits and experiences, you decide, as many do, that you want an Irish Wolfhound. I have found that the experiences I described in the last paragraph clearly divide *true* Irish Wolfhound people from the rest. The Wolfhound people want one even more than they dreamed possible—they *have* to have one! This is the most difficult time, because you may not get one right away, at least not the one that will make you happy in the long run. If you can afford to have more than one hound, and have the space for them, then you could do what one impatient novice did—buy the first available puppy while waiting for the ideal one to come along. That worked in his case. I happened to know someone who had a puppy she did not want to keep. He took it and loved it while he waited for a puppy he could show to come along. Most people cannot afford, do not have the space for, or simply do not want two Irish Wolfhounds.

PATIENCE

Control your impatience to have the first available puppy, so that you can learn even more about the breed, particularly about type, temperament, and other qualities that I discuss in the chapters dealing with the development of the breed, the Standard, and breed characteristics. Now is the time to spend time at dog shows, acquiring knowledge of breeders' stock and bloodlines. Even if you never show a dog, you will want the most typical hound you can get. Virtually no one today intends to hunt wolves. Nevertheless, every Irish Wolfhound owner should have a large, powerful, rough-coated Greyhound-like dog that, as Mrs. Nagle said, you would like to have

177

At six weeks old, Witchesbroom Berwyck Uther acts as if he knows he's going to be a big winner!

This six-week-old puppy knows just where she's headed—for trouble.

by your side *if* you encountered a wolf. You may not think this matters, but as time passes, it usually does. You see more dogs, compare them to yours, and begin to have "disloyal" thoughts—that your dog could look more like some other dog you have now seen, that some other dog moves more gracefully and freely than yours, in short that your dog does not quite measure up to the powerful, Greyhound-like dog described here and that you have now witnessed in real life. Of course, no dog attains perfection; no living thing does. But there are degrees of approximation to the Standard. You want your dog to meet your expectations in that respect. Only the time and effort that experience and knowledge require can help you to most closely fulfill your expectations.

My own experience tells me that waiting will benefit you and the breed as a whole. I was most fortunate to have excellent teachers when I started out in England: Mrs. Florence Nagle, Sulhamstead Kennels; Mr. and Mrs. Leslie Jenkins, Eaglescrag Kennels; Miss Susan Hudson, Brabyns Kennels; and Mr. Tom Fidler, Mapleton Kennels. All of them devoted countless hours allowing me to watch, and to be with, their many typical hounds. Furthermore, they showed me pictures, and talked to me. I absorbed it like a sponge at first, taking it all in, asking only questions about things I didn't understand. Then, as I saw more dogs and compared different stock, I came to form judgments about what the ideal Irish Wolfhound looked like, how it moved, and how it behaved. Sadly, that invaluable experience—learning from those who had devoted most of their lives to the breed, and whose experiences or families' experiences dated back to the early years of the breed revival—cannot be duplicated today. Even more, I had the opportunity to see some "great" Irish Wolfhounds, those hounds that in living flesh approximated the closest thing to perfection that our breed Standard described. I can say unequivocally that being with those dogs, with those people, and comparing their stock made me admire the breed more, appreciate its history more, and equipped me to enjoy the hounds I acquired and in the end to do my part to fulfill my responsibility to our breed, a responsibility you too shoulder if you buy an Irish Wolfhound.

If you have met a sufficient number of responsible breeders, have spent time with actual hounds as they really live, have studied type and character, you now realize that selecting a puppy entails first choosing both a breeder and his or her stock. If you have done your work well, you know that in virtually no case can you get the puppy with the most potential. Mrs. Jenkins, who taught me so much

Seven-week-old sisters headed for mischief.

Eight-week-old with the gazehound look clearly in her eye.

180

when I was learning about Irish Wolfhounds, told me once when I wanted to buy a beautiful bitch puppy she had, "If you want a good dog, Mr. Samaha, you will have to breed your own." Naturally, we cannot all breed our own dogs, emphatically we *should not*, even though we can all put bitches to dogs and produce puppies. But Mrs. Jenkins made clear that breeders keep the best for themselves, except in rare instances.

I have occasionally let people have top dogs because I did not have the time or inclination to show or breed them at a particular time in my life. I have endured criticism—even ridicule—for doing so. One annoyed woman asked me when a bitch I sold got a top win, "Why do you *always* sell your *best* dogs?" Another man commented under similar circumstances, "Well, once again you made a fool of yourself; you didn't know which one to keep." Of course, these people did not know my reasons for selling those dogs. I have found that meeting my responsibility to the breed does not mean keeping dogs here that others may benefit from having. Beyond that, I get great personal pleasure out of seeing a dog I've bred do well. I don't need to own the dog, or take it in the ring, or bring home the ribbon to get that pleasure. However, do not expect to find many responsible breeders willing to send their "best" dogs home with you.

WHICH PUPPY, WHEN, AND HOW TO GET IT

Back to getting your puppy. If you have chosen your breeder wisely, and want the stock that that breeder has, then rely on the breeder's judgment to make several critical decisions: selecting your specific puppy; when you get your puppy; how you get your puppy; and, how to introduce your puppy to its new surroundings. Chances are you will have no choice; responsible breeders will decide these questions for you or you won't get one of their pups! Ideally, a puppy should leave its littermates after it has learned how to get along with the other puppies but before it reaches a point of adapting exclusively to other dogs. Dog psychologists have studied when this critical point arrives; most say it occurs between six and eight weeks. You will find, however, that most breeders will only reluctantly part with puppies before ten weeks, and many will not do so until twelve weeks.

Twenty years ago, breeders never let their puppies go before ten weeks; they said it was unethical to do so. Increasingly, breeders

Ten weeks old and learning how to take a show pose.

Like mother, like son, nine-week-old future champion Meadowbrook King Arthur.

make an initial "cut" in their litters at about eight weeks. Particularly if it is a "pet," you have a good chance of getting your pup at eight weeks. Those who want potential show dogs must await, in virtually all cases, the breeder's decision as to what puppy or puppies he or she will keep or which one or ones the stud owner will take. Breeders want to postpone these decisions as long as possible, since the older the pup, the more confidently breeders can predict the likelihood of its reaching its potential. These decisions used to come as a rule at ten or twelve weeks. With the advent of initial eight-week screening, breeders may well "run along" their most promising puppies for more than ten weeks—even several months in some cases. I knew I was going to have a bitch puppy by Sulhamstead Woodside Finn ex Sulhamstead Moppet. Mrs. Nagle and Miss Ellis did not finally send the puppy, Sulhamstead Mist, until she was more than four months old. They did not decide until then which bitch puppy they wanted to keep. When they did, they sent Mist to me.

Most breeders will tell you their practices with respect to picking puppies, and at what age. Most also understand your excitement about the impending decision. You do not need to remind them that you are anxiously awaiting their decisions, although most do not object to your checking with them from time to time. Remember, they want to make the right decision for themselves, for you, and also for the dogs. Breeders will usually put off such important decisions until the last minute. I wanted Sulhamstead Felix so badly that I could not stop "pestering" Mrs. Nagle, beginning in June 1972. I had convinced her that I wanted the bloodlines behind him. I had also persuaded her that I had searched all over the United Kingdom to find Sulhamstead stock but no one had any available. Each time I asked, she said, "I don't know, but I'll let you know before you return to America." Finally, she asked, "When are you returning?" I answered, "September 20." She replied, "Ring me up on the nineteenth." I did. Only then did she say she would send him—the precise date, she told me, she would decide later. He arrived in October—once again, when *she* decided! I was delighted, and my waiting was worthwhile, since he produced some good hounds for me and others and his influence still affects his descendants.

Your breeder determines which puppy you will get and when. Most breeders have strong feelings for and against shipping puppies by air, the usual practice for long distances, such as transoceanic journeys. One notable exception to flying long distances: Mrs. Nagle and her partner Mary Jane Ellis brought a group of Sulhamstead

Two nine-week-olds doing what comes naturally.

This nine-week-old has found some mischief to get into.

hounds from England to the United States on the *Queen Elizabeth 2* in the early 1970s. A caravan of vehicles met the *QE 2* in New York and drove the hounds to Killybracken Kennels in Francestown, New Hampshire. Many owners willingly drive long distances to pick their puppies up personally. Others put their trust in the airlines. I have heard heated debate over whether long journeys by car cause less stress than shorter trips by air. No one has convincingly demonstrated the superiority of either. Therefore, I advise doing what makes you feel comfortable.

I have sent out puppies, and I have had owners drive thousands of miles to collect them. Despite the stress of separation from familiar surroundings, littermates, and the breeder's familiar presence—whatever the journey following it—I have never had a puppy who did not successfully survive it. However, you can ease the shock that such a wrenching from familiar to new surroundings produces. When you get your puppy home, have a place ready where you intend to keep it. Let the puppy out to walk around, to have a drink of water if it wants it, and just generally to get a "feeling" for the place. Most will eagerly investigate the scene. I have never stopped wondering at how puppies can come across the Atlantic, or the country, hauled about in a crate, exposed to the deafening roar, totally new sights and scents, from one climatic extreme to another—California's southern coast to Minnesota's harsh, vicious cold, for example—and come out of the crate acting as if nothing out of the ordinary had happened.

Outward calm and immediate adjustment do not prove absence of stress. Quite the contrary. The separation and the journey place enormous stress on puppies. These two shocks, coupled with the period of enormous growth they have entered, particularly after twelve weeks, call for calm control. I have heard many people talk about how adjusted their puppy seemed for the first few days—they sleep well, eat well, and appear so "well behaved." About the third or fourth day, things change. The calm puppy who slept so much and behaved so well has become an energetic bundle of mischief, crying, romping, and acting so much more "normal." I have always taken this initial calm to indicate the effects of the stress brought on by separation, travel, and new surroundings.

Energy, mischief-making, and generally heightened activity signal that the puppy has adjusted successfully. You can minimize the stress and hasten a healthy adjustment by insuring no more new stress than necessary. Don't change the food or the feeding patterns

Ten-week-old puppies soon to leave for new homes and families.

Twelve-week-old litter sisters i
an unusual position, *patient*
waiting for their owner (th
author) to say "Come." The
were following my command t
"Stay."

186

your breeder used for at least a week. Don't rush your puppy to the vet for a "health check" for at least two weeks, unless an emergency demands it. If you can get your vet to make a house call—believe it or not, some do—all the better. Do not worm your puppy for a few weeks. Do not take your puppy on "new" excursions for a week or so. There will be time enough for all this later. Let it get fully over the separation and the trip, and become familiar with you, your family, and other regular visitors. Of course, use your common sense. Don't overprotect your puppy for too long. I suggest at least two weeks, but if you sense good adjustment and familiarity before then, go out into the larger world sooner. If adjustment has not taken place in two weeks, wait a little longer.

Most of all, get to know your puppy, and equally important, get your puppy to know and to rely on you. These initial days and weeks provide you with an invaluable opportunity to form close ties with your dog. Take advantage of the opportunity provided by the precarious and dependent condition your puppy is in following separation and the introduction to new surroundings. That puppy needs to transfer attachments from littermates and breeder. The transfer should be to you; it will be to you. Let the puppy rely on you to guide it through the new situations, to see you with the food, with the comforting voice, with the treats, and generally the affection that Irish Wolfhounds naturally crave and need. Once formed, these ties can last throughout your dog's life.

Irish Wolfhounds can, and most of them readily do, accept, trust, and become loyal to new owners. Mrs. Nagle taught me early on that you keep no more dogs than you can personally know and care for, even if you can afford kennel staff. Put the excess hounds in good homes. After all, she pointed out, is it better to keep too many hounds kenneled, or to find them homes where they are the center of attention? I have always followed that rule to the letter. Irish Wolfhounds never forget their first owners, who successfully helped them through the separation and initial adjustment to life without mother and littermates. I have had dogs who have lived with me for one, two, or sometimes three or four years and then went to live with new owners.

The naive and inexperienced have expressed great skepticism, and sometimes sharp criticism, concerning my practice in transferring older dogs. Despite all this, I have only had one dog who did not make that adjustment successfully. They accept, trust, and remain loyal to their new owners. However, whenever I visit, they

Witchesbroom Cauldron (Eng. Ch. Witchesbroom Wizard ex Witchesbroom Magic), eight years old, and granddaughter Witchesbroom Medea, four months (Witchesbroom Law ex Witchesbroom Soloxa).

recognize me immediately, holding no grudge. Perhaps that is because they have always gone to loving homes where they received more attention than I could provide them, given that I have a family to raise and other hounds to rear and love. I think these happy reunions between first owners and their hounds demonstrate the power of those initial days and weeks spent with Irish Wolfhound puppies, separated from mother, littermates, and all familiar surroundings. Seize the opportunity of that time; make the most of it; you will never regret it.

8

Feeding and Training Irish Wolfhounds

THE IMAGINATION alone restricts the ways owners and breeders feed and train Irish Wolfhounds. Here, I provide some general ideas, drawn from the practices of a variety of breeders and owners both here and in England. No *single* proper way to feed and train Irish Wolfhounds exists. Owners and breeders have reared healthy, sound, admirable hounds according to dramatically different practices.

FEEDING

The wide variety of available foods—and feeding plans—presents choices that may well confuse and perplex novice owners. From every individual you ask about feeding, you are likely to receive a different recommendation. Feelings run strong on the subject. The remarks in the following paragraphs refer to foods that manufacturers claim—and the claim appears on their labels—provide complete diets for growth, maintenance, reproduction, lactation, or stress. Manufacturers have tested these foods extensively across many breeds for a long time against the National Research Council's recommendations for nutritional requirements. In England, twenty years ago, these complete dog foods were rare. My dogs, as did most others, ate kibble—broken cracker–type food—that contained the approximate nutritional value of good bread. To the kibble we added meat, milk, eggs, fat, and so on. No preservatives needed, no additives supplied. It was a "natural," perfect food. Manufacturers no longer produce this "incomplete" kibble.

Owners will tell you that particular brands of "complete" foods, or varieties within a brand, have ruined or, alternatively, have dramatically improved everything from coats, bone, and muscle to energy, alertness, and temperament. No doubt food plays a critical role in all these fundamentally important areas. Who can deny that what we put into our dogs' bodies on a regular basis affects their physical and mental qualities? Attributing a specific hound's makeup to a particular food, however, requires that we know that the food *caused* the characteristic. We don't—and can't—know that. Heredity plays its part; most foods are too similar to allow a distinction of sufficient precision to make such a conclusion, and too many combinations of basic nutrients produce similar results to claim that one combination wrecked, or improved, any quality. Furthermore, most major dog-food companies have tested their foods so that they work for most dogs—it's most profitable to do so. Moreover, despite the various recipes, all these foods resemble each other much more than the company's advertisements suggest. After all, it's in their interest to convince you that their food surpasses the competition.

In my experience, these strong claims about either the dangers or benefits derived from particular foods amount to harmless nonsense. Irish Wolfhounds can derive good nutrition from a wide variety of specific foods. Does this mean that you can feed Irish Wolfhounds *anything* without worrying? No. There are a few important guidelines to follow. We do have to worry about *pushing* the already aggravated growth rate of our puppies. Hence, do *not* feed puppies foods that manufacturers have designed specifically for puppies, or the high-protein varieties designed for adults under whatever name the companies give them. Feed your puppies the variety intended for maintaining an adult hound. Feed them this until, and unless, they get too fat. If they do, either feed them less or shift to the lower-calorie varieties. Second, never give puppies calcium or other vitamin and mineral supplements, particularly if you are feeding them any of the commercial dog foods, which the manufacturers have already laced with additives. In virtually all instances, a healthy

Sire (Ch. Brabyns Seskinore), dam (Ch. Meadowbrook Berwyck Patiens), and progeny (Berwyck Eudora). *Bev Stobart*

Bearflag Dunkerron (Ch. Bearflag Magmellan Seneschal ex Bearflag Kilmirra), a quality yearling, Best Puppy IWCA Specialty, 1989. Bred and owned by Jack and Judi Orsi, Bearflag Kennels, Canada; handled by Jack Orsi.

puppy will do well on the maintenance variety of any commercial dog food throughout its life. Third, see how much water your dogs drink. This tells you how much salt the food contains. I have switched from one brand to another of the "snobby" dog foods described below because the dogs consumed so much water. As soon as I switched, the dogs drank at least 40 percent less water! Dogs do not need to work their kidneys that hard just so they can eat more palatable foods.

All this means: don't worry about which specific food to choose among all those that passionate, sincere owners recommend. Probably any, or all of them, will provide your dog with a more than adequate diet. Choose any of the following types of food that suits your budget, tastes, and convenience. At one time or another, I have tried all the types, varieties, and methods of feeding described here. I have noticed no significant difference among them. My dogs have done well on all of them; I prefer one type, but for purely personal reasons that I will set out below.

GROCERY-STORE-VARIETY COMPLETE FOODS

The grocery-type total foods you see on any supermarket shelf fall into two categories—the local varieties and the national brands. Local foods vary too much to discuss here. If local small manufacturers produce them, their specific ingredients will vary depending on what the producer finds economical at the time. The large national companies maintain a more stable recipe. Since they are able to buy enormous quantities of ingredients when prices favor doing so, their foods tend to remain the same over long periods of time. This may be good. However, changing recipes provides variety for your dog, and surely won't hurt it. Manufacturers may change specific ingredients for market purposes, but they rarely alter the nutritional balance in the recipe. For example, they may replace corn with soy because locally soybeans are cheaper at the time than corn, but they will retain the recipe's proportions of protein, carbohydrates, and fats.

THE SNOBBY COMPLETE FOODS

Many owners and breeders use the growing number of expensive foods that only special pet-food supply houses sell. I call these

Witchesbroom Berwyck Uther, the 1989 IWCA Specialty Best of Breed winner, and the author in a quiet moment of mutual admiration.

foods "snobby" foods. They will nourish your dogs at a high price; I doubt that they will nourish them *better* than the cheaper grocery-store-type complete dog foods. I have used several of these snobby foods. I still do. Like too many Americans, I have extended the doubtful rule that "you get what you pay for" to the ludicrously foolish "the more you pay, the better the product." Is it any wonder that an English friend once complained, "You Americans have more money than sense." My dogs have done well on these foods; perhaps their greatest benefit is that dogs produce less waste from them—you pick up less. However, never fall for the ridiculous claim that this lesser quantity of stool reduces the cost of these foods significantly. My dogs eat as much of this food as they do the cheaper grocery-store foods. Do I still feed this snobby food? Of course. Do I think it *really* makes a difference? Except for the sodium levels I referred to earlier, of course not! Why do I do it then? Because I have more money than sense—which does not necessarily mean that I have money to throw away.

THE YUPPIE COMPLETE FOODS

The third type of food, another expensive food but with the real appeal that it does not contain preservatives and nonnutritional additives, I call "Yuppie" food. It calls to mind many of the people who patronize a local gourmet market where I shop regularly. These foods, increasing in number, are not just expensive; most are outrageously so. No one doubts the appeal of "natural" foods. However, the results from these foods do not *seem* to match the claims made for them. How can you put fat in food without preserving it? Does meat or any other animal or dairy product that has been dehydrated, cooked to death, or subject to any other process differ significantly in quality and nutritional value from ordinary grocery-store foods or snobby foods? I doubt it. My dogs showed no difference when I fed several types of this food, except that they produced *more* stools.

HIPPIE DOG FOOD

This leads me to the fourth diet for your dog—freshly cooked food. I call this the "hippie" diet because it reminds me of the patrons in the vegetarian restaurants I frequent. This type of feeding allows

After winning the brace class at the 1951 IWCA Specialty under Miss Croucher, Ch. Finn Mac Cool of Ambleside and Kinsale of Boroughbury forged through to Best Brace in Show at Harbor Cities KC under the renowned George Steadman Thomas. Ben Brown handled the well-matched pair. *Joan Ludwig*

This historic group from the 1957 IWCA Specialty includes (from left) Suzanne Rowe's Ch. Owen of Killybracken, Winners Dog and Best of Opposite Sex, handled by Lloyd W. Case; judge William W. Brainard, Jr.; and Ch. Sweet Kathy of Kilrain, Best of Breed, with owner Mary Britcher.
William Brown

you to control what you feed your dog, to prepare it, and to observe the results of your work. Several recipes for these home-prepared diets have appeared from time to time. I do not reproduce them here. Get *The Collins Guide to Dog Nutrition* by Donald R. Collins, D.V.M. (Howell Book House) if you want a good book on the subject. This type of feeding will appeal to few people living in the fast-food-grazing 1990s. It takes time, considerable work, and it is expensive. Furthermore, how "natural" are these diets? Can you control what growers have put in the ingredients? Are you going to buy "organic" grain, range-fed beef, lamb, pork, and chickens, and the latters' eggs? Can you even find these products? I have fed this diet to pregnant and lactating bitches and to young puppies. Once, I even fed newborns a recipe I designed—goat's milk, egg yolks, honey, and purified water. If I had the time, I would still do it. Would I do it because I know the dogs will *do* better on it? No. Why, then? Because it would make *me feel* better, knowing that I had reduced the sodium and some adulterations that all living things ingest in the normal course of events.

METHODS OF FEEDING

These remarks indicate that owners can comfortably choose the type of food that suits their individual budget, tastes, and life-style. The same applies to the feeding methods, of which three predominate.

Scheduled Feeding

Scheduled feeding predominates among owners of one or two dogs, although large kennels also use this system. At a scheduled time, or times (usually once, less frequently twice, and I have even heard three times) each day, the dog receives a specific amount of food. Owners may feed it dry, lightly tossed with warm water, or drenched in water and soaked for a considerable period to let it "expand," the latter on one or a combination of three *theories:* that dogs digest soaked food more easily and more completely; that it prevents or reduces the chances of bloat; that it makes the food more appetizing. I emphasize "theory" because no one *knows* that soaking does any of these things for all or most dogs. Hence, I suggest you

Ch. Brogan of Hillaway (Ch. Fair Fingal of Ambleside ex Bridie of Ambleside), owned and bred by Helen Dalton and Catherine Cram, was Best of Breed at the 1959 IWCA Specialty.

do what makes *you* feel best, unless you get some hard evidence that suggests that you do otherwise. Scheduled feeding usually means that your dog has access to the food for only a short time. If your dog does not eat within that time, then you take the food away and offer him or her nothing until the next scheduled feeding.

Free Feeding and Self-Feeding

In the second feeding method—free feeding—you measure a daily ration and allow the dog the whole day to consume the food. In self-feeding, the dog has access to as much food as it wants twenty-four hours a day. You fill whatever container you feed in (there are specially constructed feeders that hold up to fifty pounds of dry dog food), making sure that it never becomes empty. In both scheduled and free feeding, *you* choose the amount of food the dog gets. In scheduled feeding, *you* choose both the *amount* your dog eats and *when.* Your *dog* gets to choose *when* to eat in free feeding; in self-feeding, your *dog* chooses both *when* and *how much* to eat.

In most cases, all three methods work equally well, although you will hear strong preferences, often accompanied by strong claims that the dogs do best on a particular method. In the end, I think the choice depends on the wishes and feelings of the owners more than on what method most benefits the dog. I have used all three methods; they all have their strengths and weaknesses, but mostly for the owner, not the dog. Scheduled feeding gives the owner most control; for people who like control, that's good. It also permits you to determine your dog's appetite. One way to find out how your dog feels is how hungry it is. Hence, feeding time gives you the opportunity to check your dog regularly. There are, of course, other ways to monitor your dog's health; it does not depend on scheduled feeding. Finally, many people simply like to mix their dog's food and feed it to them. It provides a happy, pleasant experience for both owner and dog. Americans love to eat; their dogs usually do too. Scheduled feeding gives you the opportunity to share this pleasure with your dog.

At the other extreme stands self-feeding. Owners who self-feed their dogs do not control when or how much is eaten. Ordinarily, they cannot determine from day to day how much their dogs eat. Most derive little or no pleasure from occasionally spying their dogs

Ch. Ballykelly Colin, owned by Mrs. H. Sheppard Musson and bred in Ireland by Sheelagh Seale, enjoyed a very successful career in the United States. This hound became a multiple Best in Show winner and is pictured here being awarded Best of Breed at the 1967 IWCA Specialty under judge Kenneth Given; the handler is Clint Harris. *William Gilbert*

Ch. Talgarth of Ambleside, owned by Killybracken Kennels, shown here being awarded Best Hound at the Danville (Illinois) KC under Frank Ward. He is handled by Mrs. C. Groverman Ellis. *Frasie*

crunching a bit of dry food from an aluminum feeder. Hence, self-feeding is rarely a novice owner's method of choice. However, it has its advantages. Surely, it is most convenient, both for you and your dog. You fill the feeder, your dog empties it at will. Second, your dog eats when it's hungry, not when you decide it should eat. Third, your dog's appetite will naturally adjust to the animal's actual needs. As the weather cools, your dog will eat more, especially if it spends most time outside in cold climates. In extreme winters, fifty-pound feeders will empty within a few days. In hot, humid summers, a dog may take more than ten days to empty the same feeder. Similarly, a largely sedentary dog that spends most of the time lolling about your house will nibble only a little food from time to time, unlike most human couch potatoes who will lie about eating all day. An active dog who has had a five-mile walk, a long gallop on a flood plain, over rough mountainous terrain, or who has coursed a lure or jack rabbit will eat considerably more. Your dog will decide how much more.

One warning: you cannot self-feed a glutton. No one has collected numbers as to how many gluttonous Irish Wolfhounds exist. I have had only one in ten years. Other breeders estimate about the same number. The only way to determine whether you have a glutton is to put the dog on self-feeding and monitor its weight. You will know within a few weeks whether your dog is putting on excess weight. And a final note. If you have been schedule-feeding your dog and decide now that you would like to try self-feeding, don't get discouraged by an initial splurge of eating in which most dogs indulge when first introduced to self-feeding. They will adjust quickly.

Free feeding provides an excellent solution for the gluttonous dog whose owner does not want to mix and feed on schedule. You can also use free feeding to gradually introduce your dog to self-feeding. Put the amount of food you would ordinarily feed your dog on schedule in a bowl every day for a few days, and then fill the feeder. That should eliminate most problems in shifting from scheduled to self-feeding.

The Finicky Eater

Gluttony due to a dog's natural bent and to overfeeding have easy solutions—cut down on the amount your dog eats. More frustrating, and far more common among Irish Wolfhounds who live inside without other dogs, is the problem of the finicky eater, which

Ch. Brian Boru of Edgecliff is shown here taking Best in Show at Pasadena in 1950. This historically interesting photo includes judge Walter Reeves, a legendary all-rounder and a great friend of Irish Wolfhounds; owner Thomas B. Wanamaker, Jr.; and handler, the colorful Harold Duffy. *Deo Paul*

Ch. Sean Craig of Ambleside (Sean O'Toole of Skyline ex Ch. Mona Craig of Ambleside), owned by Kennett W. and Dorothy H. Patrick and bred by Alma J. Starbuck, was Best of Breed at the West Coast Specialty in 1959 and 1960. He is shown here in a win under Mrs. Ramona Van Court Jones; the handler is Yvonne Chashoudian.

Joan Ludwig

understandably bothers many novices; it also upsets far too many longtime owners who should know better. There are several reasons why dogs don't eat what, or all, that's put before them. Let me assure you that the chronically finicky eater is almost never sick or injured. Your vet can easily rule out those two reasons. If your dog is neither sick nor injured, I promise you that your adult dog will not stand by and voluntarily starve to death, nor will your puppy suffer irreparable damage by not eating what and how much you think he or she should eat. Adults dogs that do not eat how and what you think they should usually have no appetite because they do not *need* to eat. They have used few calories, they have not gotten their activity level up enough to eat. Happily, unlike humans, they don't eat because they're bored. Puppies usually get finicky because owners fret, worry, and offer them too much too often.

I suggest that with many finicky eaters, the owner, not the dog, has the problem. In the first place, how do we define "proper" weight? What is a "thin" dog? I submit that most of us want our dogs too heavy for their own good. Thin dogs worry us, and they surely displease too many judges, but your dog will suffer far fewer health problems from carrying too little weight than from carrying too much. Try to redefine your concept of thin. Think "Greyhound-like," a dog that should look like a galloping hound. That will help. Furthermore, tell yourself repeatedly that a thin dog usually does not have a health problem. Get your dog—and yourself—outdoors into the air. Find a place to let your dog run, as on a flood plain or over rough mountain terrain, by an ocean, or just around city parks or country roads. Burn up calories, get both of your metabolic rates up. When you come home and have a shower and your dog has a chance to rest, you'll both be hungry. This will solve many finicky eaters' problems.

For some finicky eaters, you will probably have to do a little more than get them out and exercised, although dogs who live outdoors are rarely finicky eaters. When I bought Sulhamstead Felix, I asked Mrs. Nagle how and what to feed him. She answered curtly, and wisely, "Felix has learnt to eat what's put before him." Your dog will almost surely do the same. I recommend the following plan in addition to exercise and outdoor living. If your dog doesn't eat, never coax. Simply remove the food. Feed him nothing for twenty-four hours. Then offer your dog a half-cup of food. If he eats that amount, fine. But feed no more for another day. This too is critical—you want your dog to be hungry. You will not starve your dog by doing this.

English and American Ch. Boroughbury Brona, bred by Elsie James and owned by Samuel Evans Ewing III. An IWCA Specialty winner and multiple Best in Show winner, she is shown scoring a Group first under Robert Waters; she was handled by Mr. Ewing. *Evelyn M. Shafer*

Ch. Caragahoolie O'Killybracken, bred by Doris Hunt and owned by Killybracken Kennels, was also a Specialty and multiple Best in Show winner. This hound was guided by Roberta Campbell, who is shown with him in a Group win under Marjorie Siebern. *Stephen Klein*

The next day, and this is critical, offer the same amount. If he eats it, wonderful—but offer no more! On the third day, raise the amount to a cup. If he eats it, great, but offer no more. Keep gradually increasing the amount daily with *nothing* but water in the meantime as long as your dog eats everything in the dish. Don't ever feed your dog more than he will *eagerly* and *immediately* eat. You will have solved your finicky eater's problems. If the dog does not eat the half-cup of food, and is not sick or injured, remove the food and do not feed the dog for another day. Eventually, your dog will eat— remember, Irish Wolfhounds without disease or injury will not voluntarily starve!

TRAINING

Follow the suggestions here, and I think you will successfully train your Irish Wolfhound with a minimum of frustration and disappointment. First, decide what you expect from your dog. Before obtaining an Irish Wolfhound, make a list of the things that will please or bother you. Remember that a dog whose behavior pleases you will be the greatest companion you will ever have. One that engages in behavior that displeases you will be a constant source of irritation, frustration, and unhappiness. In both the Irish Wolfhound's and your own interest, you must have a hound whose behavior pleases you.

Second, don't impose unrealistic expectations on your hounds, particularly puppies. Keep in mind some basic facts. All puppies, whatever their breed, chew, dig, play rough, and get into what humans call mischief. Since Irish Wolfhounds are much bigger, and stay puppies much longer, they will dig much bigger holes, chew much more extensively, and make much bigger "messes" than other puppies over an extended period of time. Furthermore, for a considerable time after they look like they are grown up, they remain puppies. I have purposely kept the effects of puppy activity for people interested in Irish Wolfhounds to view for themselves.

A once-beautiful, mature apple tree that produced magnificent fruit now stands black, barren, and dead because a four-month-old puppy stripped all the bark from its trunk from the ground up to a height of four feet. A picnic table with no top graced our back lawn after I looked out the window to see two four-month-old puppies happily running around with the planks that used to be its top in their mouths. At any time, kennel yards contain at least a few un-filled holes at least three feet in diameter and often more than two feet deep. I have had puppies—and adults—dig a cave so deep in the side of a steep hill that an adult Irish Wolfhound could walk inside and totally disappear from sight.

You cannot alter this behavior. It comes with being an Irish Wolfhound puppy. Like children and teenagers, they grow out of it. You can "roll with these punches" until your puppy outgrows these stages, although many hounds never outgrow digging. Or you can try to get some pleasure out of them. If you can't do either of these things, you probably should get an adult hound, or consider another breed.

Turning to the things you can control, at a minimum a hound whose training includes the following satisfies most people: house-breaking, comfortably accompanying you on a lead wherever you go, coming when called, being left alone, staying in another room while you entertain friends within your hound's sight and hearing. Because of its character and appearance, an Irish Wolfhound that does all of these things provides an unending source of pleasure, pride, and fulfillment for you during the hound's entire life. If you require a lot more, consider another breed.

Third, I recommend that you make it easy for your dog to behave according to your expectations, and difficult for it to do otherwise. Try always to be in the position of praising your dog's desired behavior, and avoid having to punish your dog for engaging in behavior that you do not want. I always try to discover my dogs doing what I want so that I can praise them, and not to catch them in prohibited acts that I have to punish. In getting your hound to conform to your rules, an ounce of prevention is truly worth several pounds of cure.

Housebreaking

I have kept several dog breeds in the last forty-five years, and in my experience the Irish Wolfhound is the most easily housebroken of all of them. Adult hounds who have lived in kennels seem not to need training. Ordinarily, they don't "go" in the house; they wait until they get outside. Your job is easy with adult hounds used to living kenneled outside. You simply make sure you put them out first thing in the morning, a few times during the day, and then last thing at night. I have brought many hounds inside, followed this pattern, and never had a problem. However, you should probably not allow your hound to roam freely about the entire house until you are sure there will be no problems. Select a "safe" place in the house, one without carpets or bare wood that absorbs urine. Close your dog in that room or area for a few days or a week whenever you're out. That should be all that's necessary.

Housebreaking puppies takes more work, but should occur fairly quickly. I have had many puppies who have never had an "accident," using the following method. I *always* make sure I take a puppy outside to the same area at the following times: whenever a puppy wakes up after sleeping (you can even wake your puppy up if you like); after eating, and following any activity. I *never* bring my puppies in until they "go." I always praise them, affectionately handle them, and give them something they love to eat (cheese, particularly some strong cheddars, which every Irish Wolfhound I've known has loved). I *always* bring the puppy inside immediately. The trick is to make it easy to do what you want—go outside—and difficult to do what you don't want—go inside. Puppies always urinate when they wake up; they frequently urinate and defecate after eating and exercise. If you make sure they can follow this natural pattern outdoors, you will have little trouble housebreaking your puppy, frequently without a single accident.

Until I have totally housebroken puppies who live in the house, I never leave them unattended in a whole house, or even an entire room. I have taken Irish Wolfhound puppies to my office, following the rules I mentioned. I have left puppies in my car for hours, coming out to check on them frequently. Of course, I always take precautions to make sure they won't suffocate or freeze in the car—and so must you if you follow my advice here. I take them out of the car every few hours for a walk and to "go." Within a few days, they are not only housebroken, they have become familiar with all sorts of places and people. The good and the bad from this practice: for the rest of their lives, they love to accompany you when you go out, and they are comfortable doing so, *but*—they will forever dislike being left behind.

People say to me, "This is easy for you to do because you can arrange your own hours, be where you want when you want, and come and go as you please. What about people who have to go to work and stay there all day?" I have known numerous people with jobs such as this. Most have worked it out. One man took his puppy to the plant where he worked, and left it in his car. On breaks and at lunch, he took his puppy out for a walk, and within a week he could leave it at home in a restricted area. Those who live close to work have gone home during the day to walk the puppy. Others have planned their vacation around the puppy's arrival—an excellent idea. Still others have puppy-sitters to get them through these critical days. Whatever it takes to housebreak your puppy, you will not regret doing it. Irish Wolfhounds make enormous "messes." You really don't want to clean them up. Remember, housebreaking lasts for life. Once it is accomplished, you can relax about it for all your dog's days. You'll be happier; so will your dog.

Lead Training

Irish Wolfhounds learn quickly and easily to walk on a lead. I recommend the following procedure. I have lead-broken most puppies within minutes using this method, but it's best to spread these minutes over several days. The first day, put a collar on the puppy without a lead. Let the puppy get used to the collar. He will scratch at it, move in weird directions, and generally not like the collar for a little while. Take it off after a few minutes. The next day, or whenever he has accepted the collar, put the lead on. Let him either drag it about or hold the lead and follow him wherever he goes. Do *not* restrain or direct him with it. After a few minutes, take it off. The next day, put the lead on again and follow him about for a minute or two. Then call him to you, praise him, give him affection and a food treat. Now take a few steps; if he follows, give some tension to the lead, but only a little, talking to him the whole time. If he resists, let go and call him to you. When he moves toward you, create a little tension on the lead. Usually, he will come to you now. I have found that except in rare instances this works, and quickly. The idea is to follow the puppy at first until the lead does not feel uncomfortable or strange to him. Then gradually guide him on the lead a little at a time.

Most puppies will ease into the lead within a few minutes using this method. Furthermore, they will usually do so happily. I do not use the method that some do—dragging the puppy along until it learns that following you releases the tension and ends its discomfort. I think it takes longer, and the puppies really dislike it. I am sure it does not *ruin* them, but why subject your puppy to an unpleasant method when a pleasant one works better.

They can get birds, too. Two Ambleside Hounds after a successful pheasant hunt.

A group of Rathmullan Wolfhounds form up behind Alex Scott for some coursing near
Alex's Santa Fe, New Mexico home.

9

The Irish Wolfhound in Obedience, Coursing, and Conformation

TRAINING A DOG of any breed must take into account the nature of the breed, the temperament of the individual dog, and the kind of training you plan to undertake. With the Irish Wolfhound, remember that you will make more progress in a climate of mutual trust and respect than by insisting on knife-edge responses. If you bear this in mind, you can expect good results in training your Irish Wolfhound for Obedience, coursing, or conformation competition.

OBEDIENCE

Housebreaking and lead training both form part of obedience. Beyond them, the activities can get quite complex. How much more complex constitutes a highly controversial subject among Irish Wolfhound owners. Passions run high both as to *how* obedient Irish

Wolfhounds should be and *what* commands Irish Wolfhounds should learn to obey. Irish Wolfhounds are not Dobermans or German Shepherds. Never expect your hound to respond with the quick, precise, almost reflex action that these breeds do. Irish Wolfhounds tend to be more deliberate and laid-back in their response. If you can't live with this, find another breed. I heard of a Doberman stud whose owner commanded, "Mount!" The Dobe instantly mounted. The owner then commanded, "Penetrate!" The Dobe instantly complied. The owner followed with the command, "Thrust and tie!" The Dobe unfailingly complied. I did not hear whether the owner commanded his bitches to "Release!" once sufficient time to ejaculate had elapsed. I am not sure I would want a Doberman—or any dog—to respond so unflinchingly to my commands. It wouldn't matter if you or I wanted an Irish Wolfhound to so respond. They will not. They should not! These are living creatures, not machines.

I feel the same about the *degree* of compliance. Some owners expect their hounds to obey all the time, without fail, to all their commands. I don't expect such perfection. Neither should you. Both you and your dog will be happier if you can live with something less than perfection. Also, I think you can deceive yourself, sometimes dangerously so, by thinking that your dog will always obey. I know of people who will tell you their dogs accompany them everywhere without leads, including crossing busy streets, alongside freeways. In fact, I used to be such an owner. I had trained my first Irish Wolfhound, Sanctuary Peggeen, to come, stay, heel, and wait for me indefinitely outside buildings. She always accompanied me to UCLA, where I was teaching at the time. She went everywhere with me. When she could not enter a building, such as the library, she waited outside for me. She was always there when I returned.

It was great—this obedient, loyal, dependable dog who wanted to be with me and who was content to wait for me when I left, all without any restraint. It was also stupid, and I was lucky that my stupidity neither lost, injured, nor killed my dog. Someone could have stolen her; in those days in the 1960s people did steal Irish Wolfhounds, and sold them. Their owners rarely heard about them afterwards. Furthermore, she could have been injured or killed. Never think that your dog will follow you everywhere without restraint. You must remember that they are animals, sighthounds by breeding and heredity. Something may catch their eye, triggering the need to chase. Do not flatter yourself into believing loyalty to you and the power of your training will overcome this need. It won't. Nor

Ch. Killary of Ambleside (left) and his daughter Ch. Merry of Rathain, owned by Charles D. Burrage, Jr. Killary is the paternal *and* maternal grandsire of the American export, English Ch. Rory of Kihone, owned by the Sanctuary Kennels and sent over to help the postwar gene pool.

will it keep your hound from harm's way. Running across a highway or into a crowded street may well lead to your hound's death. I was lucky. You can prevent this from ever happening by keeping your hound on a lead and not allowing it to remain unattended where someone may steal or hurt it.

What commands should your hound obey? I have recommended that it come, sit, stay, and remain in a room when you are nearby. These commands make it possible for you to live with your hound without undue frustration and unhappiness. You can either teach your hound all these, and much more, informally at home, or formally at obedience school. Furthermore, you can also train your hound to obey commands that make it easier and pleasanter to live with. You can also make obedience a major aspect of the hound's activity and social life. Some owners want to take their hounds into Obedience competition. This aspect of obedience generates considerable controversy.

Some people wax passionate on the subject of Obedience competition—some for, others equally heatedly against. Those who favor Obedience competition think that it is fun for both them and their dogs, that it's more interesting than conformation, that it challenges both owner and dog, and that the dogs love it. Those opposed maintain that Obedience competition does not comport with the character of the Irish Wolfhound. Irish Wolfhounds are not like German Shepherds and Dobermans, hence not amenable to high-precision instant responses. Furthermore, they claim that Obedience competition demeans Irish Wolfhounds by forcing them to perform "undignified tricks." The requirements of Obedience competition are no more useful or dignified, according to critics, than making dogs jump through hoops, bring slippers to their masters, or fetch newspapers.

You must decide for yourself what you want from your hound. You can find plenty of people who will urge you to compete in Obedience trials for the reasons mentioned above. Some will maintain that your dog will somehow be lacking if it does not get highly trained. This, of course, is not true. On the other hand, you will find plenty of people who will tell you that you will "wreck," even *mistreat*, your hound if you subject it to Obedience competition. Neither of these extremes is true. I think you can find other ways than, or in addition to, Obedience competition to make your hound complete, whatever that means. I am satisfied with my hounds as long as they go with me wherever I want to go, come when I call, stay by themselves when I am gone, and do not foul my house. Their character and looks do more for me than any trained acts they could perform. On the other hand, I have seen Irish Wolfhounds whose success in Obedience competition did not wreck their spirits.

COURSING

Coursing, like Obedience, has its strong advocates and equally passionate critics. Coursing falls into two categories: live and lure. In live coursing, as its name indicates, the hounds run after real animals, usually jackrabbits. The hounds go to the jackrabbits' habitat, and the hounds run in more or less natural circumstances. Live coursing spawns the most controversy; some who accept lure coursing will not tolerate live coursing. Some people simply cannot approve of hunting live animals for sport. Others condemn live coursing because jackrabbits are not enough like wolves to test the hounds' capacity to catch and bring down dangerous prey. Jackrabbits run differently, turn differently, and act according to a different psychology and physiology than wolves. Hounds who can catch wolves do not necessarily need the same qualities that catching jackrabbits entails.

Lure coursing is artificial. A lure on the end of a wire follows a course designed and set up by those running the match. A motor pulls the lure through the course. The course is specifically set up to test straight runs and turns. The judges measure the hounds' capacity to stay with the lure, take the turns properly, and run with it.

Coursing is beautiful to watch. To see Irish Wolfhounds galloping, turning, hunting in the field, tests their power, speed, and agility. Furthermore, it shows the hounds doing more or less what they originally were bred to do. On the other hand, coursing, particularly lure coursing, quickly bores most Irish Wolfhounds. In addition, coursing subjects hounds to the possibility of injury.

Coursing will dilute type if those who course their hounds do not keep in mind the Standard of the Irish Wolfhound. People whose dogs run with the other sighthounds, all of whom are supposed to be more refined and smaller than Irish Wolfhounds, tend to put a premium on speed and agility. They conclude that the faster the dog, the better the hound. That simply is not true. The faster and more agile hounds tend to be small and fine boned, more like Deerhounds and Greyhounds than Wolfhounds. Remember, Irish Wolfhounds must combine power and speed—they are the tallest and most pow-

A yearling Irish Wolfhound bitch that is definitely interested in lure coursing.

Taking a curve to get the lure.

erful of the galloping hounds. To sacrifice bone and size in search of speed will quickly lead to hounds that do not meet the Standard's requirements of power, substance, *and* speed.

I have seen tremendously fast and agile Irish Wolfhounds that were too refined to meet the Standard. These may be pleasing to watch, but far more thrilling is to see a large, powerful Irish Wolfhound covering enormous ground galloping in the field. Their size, particularly length of leg, and power allow them to cover this ground more quickly even if they are larger. They can go the same distance as the smaller, lighter sighthounds with fewer strides. No greater sight have I had of Irish Wolfhounds than that of a large, powerful hound galloping across a field in that enormous double suspension gallop—folding and extending.

As long as coursing enthusiasts keep the Standard in mind, and not the other sighthounds running with the Irish Wolfhounds, they will not endanger type. If they lose sight of the Standard, their desire for speed and agility will seduce them into putting aside the requirements of size, power, and substance. This seduction is easy to understand because Irish Wolfhounds lose size, substance, and power first. The breed tends toward refinement, not coarseness. Once lost, bone and substance may be impossible to recapture. This tendency to dilute type, in my opinion, is the greatest danger that coursing poses.

CONFORMATION

Most Irish Wolfhound owners who want to participate in activities with other dogs choose conformation, not Obedience or coursing. Conformation—that is, "showing" dogs, either in formal American Kennel Club "pointed" events that lead to championships or in informal "fun matches"—is in one sense a beauty contest. Irish Wolfhounds that in the judge's opinion conform to the Standard will get the prizes. In other words, your dog competes with others to determine which one, in the judge's opinion, best fits the ideal. Chapter 6, "A Discussion of Breed Type," and the Guide to Following the Judging of Irish Wolfhounds, below in this chapter provide further development of these points.

Some advice to novices: showing your hound gives you the opportunity to compare its conformation with others in competition. Approached properly, dog shows can teach you a great deal. Go to them hoping to win; everyone likes to win. But go for other reasons too. Go to meet people, to look at their hounds, to compare yours with theirs, and to get the judge's opinion. But let me caution you about the judge's opinion. Too many judges today do not know Irish Wolfhound type. Certain judges tack on Irish Wolfhounds to the other breeds they *really* want to judge. For all-breed clubs who sponsor shows, and for judges too, group approval makes it easier, more economical, and generally more feasible than assembling judging panels. Most all-breed clubs will not "hire" judges unless they can judge enough breeds to add up to 175 dogs—the maximum number of entries allowed a judge at a single show.

In my experience, most judges in all-breed shows either know nothing about proper Irish Wolfhound type, or worse, do not care. I have found too many judges who do not even *like* Irish Wolfhounds. They make disparaging remarks about them, reveal colossal ignorance regarding their character and type, and hurry through judging the Irish Wolfhounds so that they can get to the breeds they really care about. Naturally, these judges will teach novices the wrong thing, will annoy experienced breeders and owners, and will frequently discourage owners with good hounds from showing their dogs. Mrs. Nagle expressed her exasperation with most American judges. She said, "I used to think that *any* American dog could become a champion. Now, I believe that it is impossible for a *good* dog to become a champion in America."

One, among many, reasons for this situation rests on the enormous increase in the number of all-breed shows, and the total entries at those shows. Entries that total thousands of dogs tempts American Kennel Club administrators, show superintendents, and show committees to put a premium on efficiency, economy, and speed at the expense of quality and knowledge. Perhaps equally important, uniformity in decision-making takes precedence over the content of the decision. For example, AKC representatives, commonly called "reps" (people who see to it that championship shows run according to AKC rules) seem more concerned with whether judges go over dogs at a proper rate (twenty-five dogs an hour on the average, according to rule) and in an acceptable manner (do the same thing to every dog) than they are with whether judges find the "best" dog.

While judging around the country, I have had AKC "reps" criticize my judging for a whole range of factors not related at all to selecting the best dog. I hope and believe that the AKC wants judges to pick the best dog, but I also know they feel the pressure of numbers and they understand that harmony, uniformity, and effi-

Ch. Drakesleat Roisin and Ch. Witchesbroom Wizard (Ederyn Mogul ex Witchesbroom Magic).

Ch. Fitzarran Dudly of Whitehall (Ch. Wild Isle Warlock ex Ch. Eaglescrag Kate).

ciency help to "manage" these large numbers. Selecting the right dog may well interfere with the need to administer a well-run dog show and to reduce the chances of complaints, an increasingly common occurrence as sportsmanship bows to the desire to win at all costs among too many exhibitors, particularly at all-breed dog shows.

In the end, championship shows provide the opportunity to compare Irish Wolfhounds. Knowledgeable people will sort out the dogs without the judge's help. Novices must remember that most judges who judge Irish Wolfhounds in all-breed dog shows do not know—may not even like—our breed. This lack of knowledge must discount their decisions' value to the extent that ignorance or prejudice forms it. Of course, knowledgeable all-rounders exist, and they have a major place in dog-show judging. While breeder-judges—specialists, one might call them—tend to focus on current problems or faults, knowing intimately the current state of the breed, all-rounders look at the breed with a generalist's eye. The breed needs both specialists and *knowledgeable, concerned* generalists to judge entries not only at all-breed shows but also at Specialties.

A GUIDE TO FOLLOWING THE JUDGING OF IRISH WOLFHOUNDS

I distribute this guide to exhibitors and spectators when I judge Specialties. Although written specifically to help novices to follow judging at Specialties, it should prove equally useful at all-breed shows. Several prospective judges and many exhibitors have told me that they have found it useful.

Introduction

A National Specialty brings together many dogs from all over the country and even from other countries. It affords a rare opportunity to see dogs across a wide spectrum that in their owners' judgment represent the best stock they have. Viewed from a broad perspective, these dogs enable us to assess our breed's past, present, and future. While dogs in their prime reflect the breed's present state, our deep debt to the past is also in evidence at our Specialties. We glimpse that past in the Veterans classes firsthand, and it speaks to us indirectly through the heritage displayed in pedigrees from all

Arntara Keystone Lionel (Ch. Keystone Morlyn ex Arntara Lyric).

Ch. Fleetwind Magnum (Ch. Fleetwnd Dan ex Seawing Tara).

classes. We must never forget this heritage in the powerful pull to consider only the present. Not only do we see the present and the past; in the puppies, yearlings, and novices is revealed our hope for the breed's future, the direction the Irish Wolfhound is heading. From these not-yet-mature hounds, we can assess to what extent we are fulfilling our custodial responsibility to leave the breed in at least as good a condition as we found it.

Attending a Specialty, then, is obviously a valuable opportunity to learn about our breed. But it can be overwhelming, especially to novices who wonder how best to reap the benefits from this experience. In order to help you follow the judging, I have outlined below the steps I follow in deciding where to place the dogs in each class. They are not the only steps a judge might follow, but they are the ones I have found most useful over the years. I have also included some comments about each step. I hope they will help you to understand what I am doing and why.

Use this guide and commentary not only to follow what I am doing but also to clarify your own ideas. I believe firmly that you should make your own decisions about the dogs, and I strongly urge you to do so. Everyone has an opinion. We all like some dogs more than others and have a "favorite" dog at the show. Don't be afraid to take a stand. Compare your decision with mine and consider why you prefer some dogs to others all through the judging. Finally: Which dog would you pick for Best in Show? Can you say why? I hope we can discuss some of these decisions and the reasons that lie behind them following the judging.

When you read this guide and watch the judging, try to keep four thoughts in mind:

1. *There is no absolute right and wrong.* Reasonable people will disagree about what should be given the greatest weight in judging Irish Wolfhounds. Even if they can agree on this, they may argue honestly about how to apply the Standard to particular dogs. This is no cause for distress. It renders the whole experience interesting, exciting, challenging, and even fun. When you read the Guide and when you watch the judging, think about what parts of the Standard you consider most important. A checklist at the end of the Guide is provided for you to mark your choices. We will discuss them following the judging.

2. *Nothing about Irish Wolfhounds is simple.* Some people believe a single, simple, straightforward formula exists for judging, showing, breeding, feeding, rearing, and even living with Irish Wolf-

Ch. Hope of Whitehall (Ch. Wild Isle Warlock ex Ch. Honey Voo Greta Garbo).

Fitzarran Comus (Fitzarran Kinsman ex Ch. Fitzarran Mandan), Best of Breed and Best of Winners, Irish Wolfhound Association of New England Specialty, 1988. Bred and owned by William and Betty Deemer, Jr.

Ch. Arntara Meadowbrook Hex (Arntara Legend ex Witchesbroom Hesper), Best of Breed, Northern California Irish Wolfhound Club Specialty, 1988. Bred by Mr. and Mrs. James Arn, owned by D. Arn and J. Samaha.

hounds. Anyone who believes this is simpleminded. Unfortunately, there are many things we do not yet know—others we will probably never know. To make matters still more complicated, what we do know may greatly benefit one dog while wreaking havoc on another. Hence, in the end, to most questions about Irish Wolfhounds we must accept admittedly unsatisfying answers such as, "We don't know"; "It might be A, but it could be B, or C, or even A, B, C, and X"; and so on. No one likes such vague answers to questions he so desperately wants answered. But that does not make the answers wrong.

3. *Keep an open mind.* Recognize that others might have something to say that is worth hearing. A different point of view is not always wrong. People who disagree with you are not necessarily stupid and ignorant, nor are they automatically brilliant and knowledgeable just because they like your dogs. Try to understand why someone might honestly disagree with you, and look for some merit in what they have to say. Learn to appreciate quality wherever you see it, even if (no, especially if) your fiercest rival's hound possesses it!

4. *Judging is seeking dogs who approximate an ideal.* No dog is perfect. No living thing is. Judging, therefore, must always be a compromise between reality and an ideal. In the end, a judge must choose the best dogs in real life, not the nonexistent perfect one in his or her mind's eye. The dogs in living flesh that come closest to my mind's eye picture of the perfect dog will be the winners.

The Guide

STEP 1:

Overall Impression. I form my overall impression in two stages: (1) dogs standing still, and (2) dogs in motion.

    a. *Standing Still.* The first thing I do in every class is to look up and down the line of dogs in order to assess four critical features:

        1. *Shape or outline.* Here is the first opportunity to determine which dogs fit my image of the large, rough-coated Greyhound-like dog our Standard calls for. Curves, depth of chest, length of neck, body, and leg—an impression of a large, strong galloping hound—these make up the proper outline. Another word to describe outline might be "silhouette."

Ch. Celtic Wind's Erinwood Apollo (Ch. Erinwood Brogan ex Erindale Kim), Best of Breed, Irish Wolfhound Club of Puget Sound, 1988. Bred and owned by Rod and Jill Anderson.

Brogan Solo (Ch. Kingsland Sovereign ex Brogan Honor Bright), Best of Breed, Potomac Valley Irish Wolfhound Club Specialty, 1988. Bred, owned and handled by Mildred Koschara.

2. *Quality.* It has been said that quality cannot be defined, that it speaks for itself. And so it does. Dogs who possess it stand away from the others, as if they were cast in a special mold.

3. *Presence.* Related to but not to be confused with quality, presence is an attitude. A dog with presence bears itself as if to say, "I am the one!" This dog does not plead to be first. It knows it is best and hopes you agree. If you don't, well, it's your loss. This dog has "commanding appearance."

4. *Balance.* Shape, quality, and presence are all greatly diminished if there is no balance. Balance means all the dog's parts fit together. It means curves and length, breadth and depth are proportionate. A balanced dog rests there, just as the word "balance" implies. Unbalanced dogs make you feel awkward; even the most skillful handlers cannot bend them into balance, even though the best handlers are very good at trying. Some examples of imbalance are: a long body on short legs; a very steep shoulder and curving stifles; a short neck set into a long body; long legs and shallow chest. It is important to note that a dog can be balanced and yet not typical. A short-necked, short-bodied, straight-shouldered, straight-stifled dog is very balanced (I readily admit I have owned some)—but it is not typical.

b. *In Motion.* After I get an initial impression from the dogs standing still, I ask their handlers to take them around the ring all together. Please note well that this step is not to assess sound movement. That will come later when I examine individual dogs. At this point, I am looking for the same four qualities assessed standing—shape, quality, presence, and balance—but in motion. This step is often a surprise. The dog that appears straight when standing can in motion suddenly bend into soft curves, while the hound balanced when standing can in motion look as if many parts from different dogs were all stuck together to make one animal. It is never easy to have to choose between the dog who has shape, quality, presence, and balance standing but loses them in motion and one who has them in motion but not when standing. The best hounds excel in both.

STEP 2:

Judging Individual Dogs. Once I get this overall first impression, the process of elimination—which really is what judging is—enters the second stage. I use two methods to examine individual dogs: (1) *looking* at the dog both standing and moving, and (2) *feeling,* often

Ch. Stoneybrook Mafia (Ch. Sepulcur Shamus ex Ch. Meadowbrook Minnewashta), Best of Breed, Irish Wolfhound Association of the West Coast Specialty, 1988. Bred and owned by L. and J. Simon; handled by L. Simon.

Ch. Bearflag Skeagh (Ch. Bearflag Magmellan Seneschal ex Keystone Ksan), Best of Breed, Irish Wolfhound Association of Delaware Valley Specialty, 1988. Bred by Jack and Judi Orsi; owned by D. and L. Pitteway.

227

referred to as "getting your hands on the dog." What am I looking and feeling for? Five main elements critical to assessing a dog thoroughly can only be ascertained by touching and looking:

a. *Substance.* Proper substance means the dog has sufficient bone, muscle, breadth, and depth. I am looking for a dog that combines power and speed. An Irish Wolfhound should be fast enough to catch a wolf and, once caught, strong enough to bring it down. Irish Wolfhounds must *be* strong; they must *look* strong. Typical Irish Wolfhounds are never weak or refined, nor should they even appear to be either. In my opinion, they should resemble hunters more than racers.

When you see me placing my hand around a dog's forearm, I am determining the amount of bone. When I feel the rib cage, I am determining breadth and depth of chest. At the rear, when I go over the hindquarters, I am assessing the amount and quality of critical muscle in both thigh and second thigh. There may be dogs who have too much bone and muscle—what we call coarse—but in my judgment, coarseness is not a breed problem. Refinement is much more prevalent and, if left unattended, will lead to "Deerhoundy" dogs that are not typical. Therefore, I prefer a dog with a bit too much substance rather than one with too little. I have seen too much substance only rarely in the past. Recently, I have not seen it at all.

PLEASE NOTE: This does not mean—and never should be taken to mean—that the biggest dogs, with the most bone and muscle, will win. Substance must be reckoned in concert with all other important breed characteristics!

b. *Structure.* Assessing structure means determining whether the dog is properly put together. Generally, this requires that dogs feel both good and right—that is, my hands move down and over a dog's body without encountering lumps and bumps. Specifically, it demands that the following be evaluated:
1. Head—shape, eyes, mouth, teeth and jaw, ears, whiskers
2. Front assembly—neck, shoulder, upper arm, foreleg, pastern, and feet
3. Body—depth and spring of rib, back
4. Rear assembly—croup, thighs, second thighs, stifles, hocks, and feet
5. Tail—length, thickness, set, carriage
6. Coat—harshness and thickness

c. *Soundness.* I believe typical Irish Wolfhounds must be sound in both mind and body, ensuring both correct temperament and proper movement.
1. *Temperament.* We must have strong, gentle hounds, never ag-

Ch. Kingsland Sovereign (Ch. Fitzarran Shadowfax ex Ch. Fitzarran Kingsland Koren), Best of Breed, Irish Wolfhound Club of Canada Specialty, 1988. Bred, owned, and handled by Phillippa Crowe Nielson.

Ch. Marumac Cinderella. Bred and owned by Miss Mary McBryde, Marumac Kennels, England.

gressive or shy—in my opinion, not even edgy ones. By "edgy," I mean dogs that are presently under control, but which, without their handler's guidance, would retreat, or worse.

PLEASE NOTE: I do not include ill-behaved, untrained, or inexperienced dogs in this category. While misbehavior or a lack of training or experience may detract from a dog, I never equate them with poor temperament, and they should not be (although to be sure they often are) confused with improper temperament.

An Irish Wolfhound with poor temperament is not only not sound, but it is also not typical; it cannot possess a "commanding appearance."

2. *Movement.* Four aspects are critical to judging movement: fore; aft; reach and drive or stride, overall easy and active. All are important, but a long, easy, and active stride takes precedence over the others, in my judgment. In a dog that covers ground with long strides easily, with grace and economy, I will forgive some faulty movement coming toward me and going away. In my judgment, the oft-touted cow hocks and flapping fronts are not nearly as serious as the belabored, mincing, short strides so often seen. Dogs with poor stride are not moving easily and actively; hence, they are not typical.

d. *Fine Points.* Now is the time to consider the finishing touches. The ones I consider most important and which in my opinion add to quality are: *face* (dark eyes, nice whiskers, and expression—that sad, faraway look we have all come to know and love in the Irish Wolfhound); *ears* (rose, small); *coat* (harsh, thick, close to the body); *feet* (round, toes tight and well arched); *condition* (healthy coat, good weight and muscle tone, overall thrifty with a strong constitution).

STEP 3:

The Final Judgment. After examining each dog individually, it is time to make the final judgment. It has two phases. The first is tentative. I arrange the dogs in the order I prefer them, according to decisions made in Steps 1 and 2. Keep in mind that the overall impression from Step 1 is very important but it is not everything. The dog with a beautiful silhouette is sometimes weak, refined, in poor condition, and suffers from important structural problems. These latter will always discount superior shape and soundness. Second, I ask the dogs to go around the ring together one (or sometimes two, and rarely three) last time(s). This is no mere formality; neither is

Ch. Drakesleat Kyak (Drakesleat Runen ex Drakesleat Musyk), top-winning hound *ever* in the United Kingdom. Bred, owned, and handled by Zena Andrews.

it a staged action to increase suspense and test the exhibitors' endurance. I have often rearranged dogs on this final go-around. Why? Not for movement as such. It is to find the dog who excels in shape, quality, presence, and balance both standing and in motion. Hopefully, the dog I put tentatively at the front of the line will retain the best shape, display the same quality, possess the same presence, and demonstrate equal balance in motion as it did standing still. If not, another dog may replace it. In the end, the winning dog best fits the description: *large, rough-coated, Greyhound-like dog, fast enough to catch a wolf and strong enough to pull it down.*

A FINAL WORD

Specialties should be pleasant experiences. Learning, competing, meeting new people, renewing old ties—these are all richly rewarding. While winning is exhilarating, it is not everything. Try to approach judging and competing in the spirit of a very wise person whose words cannot be improved upon: *"I take the dog I admire and hope the judge agrees; if not, well then I'll come another day."* (Told to me by Mrs. Ellis about ten years ago.)

Checklist

1. _____ Overall impression
   _____ standing _____ in motion
   _____ shape
   _____ quality
   _____ presence
   _____ balance

2. _____ Substance
   _____ bone
   _____ muscle
   _____ depth
   _____ breadth

3. _____ Structure
   _____ *front:*
   _____ neck
   _____ shoulder
   _____ upper arm
   _____ foreleg
   _____ pasterns
   _____ feet
   _____ body
   _____ *rear:*
   _____ croup
   _____ thighs
   _____ second thighs
   _____ stifle
   _____ hocks
   _____ feet

_____ *head:*

_____ eyes

_____ mouth _____ teeth _____ jaw

_____ ears

_____ whiskers

4. _____ Tail

5. _____ Soundness

_____ *temperament*

_____ *movement:*

_____ fore (coming)

_____ aft (going)

_____ stride

_____ overall easy and active

6. _____ Fine points

_____ face

_____ ears

_____ coat

_____ feet

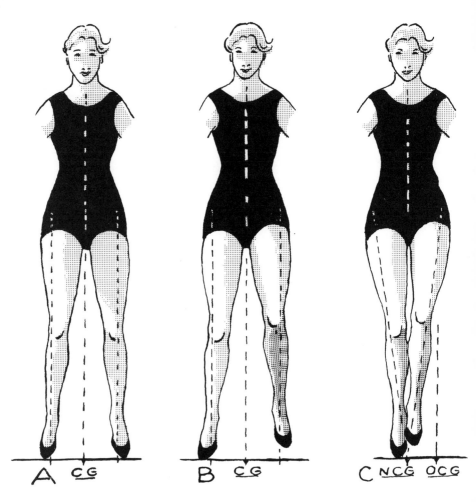

Stand as in Fig. A, with the balls of your feet as far apart as your hip sockets. Then lift the left foot (Fig. B), without swaying your body to the right, so as to bring the center of gravity over the supporting foot as shown in Fig. C, which creates a new center of gravity.

10

Wolfhound Gait

by McDowell Lyon

THE GAIT of the Irish Wolfhound is not a single factor like the color of his eyes or type of his coat but is a composite of his entire physical makeup. Except for color and markings, the other twelve sections of the Wolfhound Standard have some influence on gait and movement. The very purpose for which this dog was developed demanded efficient movement in the field, and we should maintain this as the foundation on which we continue to breed.

It was his rugged grace that first endeared the Irish Wolfhound to the sportsmen of the past. Grace and efficient movement were wed at his inception and cannot be divorced; they are as much a part of him as his size, coat, and instinct for the chase. We should keep that constantly in mind when evaluating the dogs that we see and breed.

More fallacies have clung to the ideas surrounding movement and the factors that contribute to it than to any other aspect of the dog field. This was understandable years ago, for leg action was too fast for the eye to follow it. But today the moving-picture camera has given us the answer to those enigmas, and even though with the eye alone we cannot see all that takes place, we have learned what happens and can visualize it more clearly.

Leland Stanford's desire to learn exactly what an animal's legs did when it moved, fathered experiments that began in 1872 and were carried out on the farm where Stanford University now stands. A series of twenty-four cameras was tripped in sequence by horses, dogs, deer, and other animals in their various gaits. Thomas Edison and others joined in the work, with the result that the first semblance to our moving pictures was shown at the Chicago World's Fair in 1893. From this and study following, we learned what the eye had never been able to detect before. The importance of this to us is knowing just how the legs of a Wolfhound support his body in movement, and knowing his problems of balance.

The hound starts his walk by stepping off with one front foot, followed by the opposite back foot, then the other front foot and its opposite back foot. The actual leg sequence here is the same as in the gallop, except that it is slower and the steps overlap one another so that his body is always supported partially or wholly by three legs. Therefore, maintaining balance is much easier than in the faster gaits, and can be likened to the tricycle.

The trot is known as a diagonal gait, for the right front and diagonal or opposite rear coordinate, as do the left front and its diagonal rear. This provides two legs, front and back, as support for the body and can be compared to the bicycle, which is more difficult to balance than the tricycle. Another factor that must be kept in mind when considering this is that these supports are on diagonal corners of the body and, unless the dog does something to prevent it, support would move unsteadily from side to side, causing wobbling or rolling. The dog can and does correct for this in efficient movement.

The pace is similar to the trot to a certain extent, except that it is a lateral gait where both right legs coordinate and support weight, followed by both left legs. A two-point support results, as with the trot. The dog rarely resorts to the pace unless he is very tired and leg-weary, overfat and out of condition, or is very old or very young, in which cases he is not as apt to make sufficient leg correction for support and will generally show a roll as support shifts from side to side.

In the normal or single-suspension gallop, leg sequence follows that of the walk but there is no overlapping and the body at no time is fully supported by more than one leg. A period of suspension, when all legs are off the ground, follows the straightening of the leading front leg. Sometimes two pads will appear to be on the ground, but one is leaving and the other arriving and the weight is

236

The dog faces you with feet apart, almost under the shoulder sockets, as in Fig. A. When he moves, he cannot do so as in Fig. B, with legs parallel, any more than you could hold the position of "B" as shown on page 234. He will place his pad on or near the center-of-gravity line, as in Fig. C, to maintain balance.

Some dogs swing their front legs in an arc to get the pad under the center of gravity, as though doing the Australian crawl (like the dog in Fig. A), which is a fault. A dog whose pasterns bend inward, as in Fig. B, will move close, for the pastern takes up passing space.

237

immediately taken over by the latter. This is used by the horse and by the majority of dogs, but by the Wolfhound only as a slow gallop.

The high-speed working gallop of the Wolfhound, as with other gazehounds, antelope, and cheetahs, differs from the normal gallop in that there are two periods of suspension. The Wolfhound's second one follows the straightening of the back leg opposite to the leading front leg. This latter period of suspension provides his extra comparative speed. At no time, though, does more than one leg support the body, so both styles of the gallop can be compared to the monocycle, the hardest of all cycles on which to maintain balance.

Visualizing these supports should help us gain a clearer understanding of what the Wolfhound's legs have to do and where they should be placed in reference to the body in order to maintain a balanced support with the least muscular effort. Any of us who have ever ridden a bicycle or motorcycle know that, with the exception of turns, where centrifugal force is also met, both wheels must be under the center of gravity for efficient progress.

The walk, having more leg support and being more easily followed by the eye, is responsible for some of the misconceptions harbored by some people concerning the idea of leg action. One of these major delusions is that the legs move perpendicular to the ground and parallel to one another, something like the legs on a table. Some Standards even describe gait in more or less that manner, but fortunately the Wolfhound Standard is not one of these.

A simple check should eliminate this idea from any who might harbor it. Stand with feet as far apart as the hip sockets, legs parallel, then lift one foot off the ground without shifting the body weight over the supporting foot. You will find that you have to sway the body over this base support in order to hold the other foot off the ground.

In efficient movement, the dog does not sway his body over this support but places the pad under or near the center line. So, coming toward you, the dog starts his walk with the legs relatively parallel but converges the pads toward the center as speed increases. This is true even before the gait breaks from the walk to the faster styles. One may sometimes be confused on this when watching a dog taking a turn and meeting centrifugal force, which changes the point of balance, as the dog must lean into the latter force.

The leg in all these cases should maintain a straight column of bones (when viewed from the front) from shoulder joint to pad. If this is done, the inward angle will not interfere with the passing leg that is sufficiently flexed. It is only when the pastern bends inward

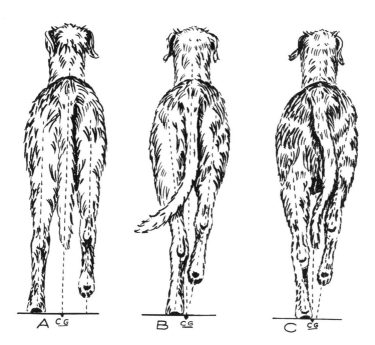

The dog cannot move away efficiently with legs parallel as in Fig. A, where he is "moving wide." The "cow-hocked" dog in Fig. B will move close, often dusting his hocks with the passing foot, and does not have a straight column of bones for body support. The efficient mover keeps the column of bones straight while placing his back pad near or on the center line, as in Fig. C, which will be in line with the front legs unless the dog is "crabbing."

or the passing leg is not flexed that the dog tends to brush the supporting leg and "moves close" in front.

It is just as faulty for the pastern to break outward as inward from this straight column of bones. This shows a weakness in the joint itself and the dog tends to run on the outside of his pad. Often this does not show when the dog is standing but is evident even to the eye when moving.

The legs should be carried straight forward from the point of the last pad contact to the next one, and the back legs should follow in the same angled plane. Some dogs may swing their legs in an arc, much like a swimmer doing the Australian crawl. All dogs try to get their support under the center of gravity even in the face of physical handicaps. Two things contribute to this swimming action: insufficient flexing of the leg moving forward, and faulty shoulder placement.

The faulty shoulder is most often placed too far forward so that it is somewhat around the front curve of the rib cage, which provides shoulder action at an angle to the spinal column or line of locomotion. The elbow is then often forced outward, the dog moving "out at the elbow." A dog may even stand true but move in this manner.

A dog has relatively the same bones and muscles as man but he lacks that one muscle which enables man to rotate the forearm. The failure to take this into consideration is responsible for another prevalent misconception, which is that when the dog is standing, his front feet should face directly forward in a position that is often described as "standing true." Being unable to rotate the forearm as it angles inward, this dog is forced to support his weight and get foot action off one center and one outside toe. The two center and stronger toes are the ones that you want in action, while the smaller toes are used on turns and to counteract side forces.

The pad that is angled outward slightly, so that you see more of the inside than the outside, will come into line on the inward swing, just as a golf club lines up with the ball on the downstroke. This will enable the dog to move over the two center toes. However, if the pad is angled outward to an extreme, it interferes with sustained movement as much as the one looking straight forward. On a plane surface, it is not difficult for the eye to detect this pad action even with the slow trot.

Watching the dog move away from you should also show a straight column of bones—from hip socket to pad. The leg will angle inward toward the center line as speed increases, moving in the same

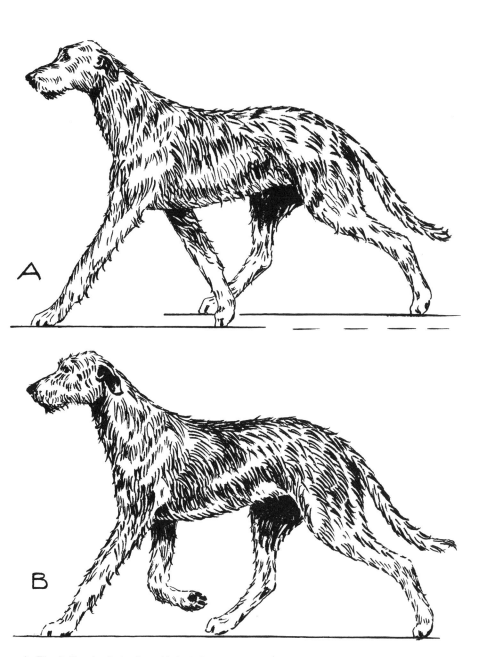

In Fig. A, the dog is trotting with both front and back feet operating in the same timing, which does not clear the weight-bearing leg out of the way of the overreaching and approaching back leg. Therefore, the dog must sidestep the front leg and will be "crabbing." In Fig. B, the dog's front feet are timed slightly ahead of the cooperating back feet. Therefore, the front foot is out of the way of the approaching back foot and allows travel in a straight line.

plane as the front leg. Deviations from either of these conditions constitute major faults. If this straight column of bone support is maintained, the passing foot, properly flexed, will have sufficient room to prevent moving close or "dusting" the supporting hock.

The inward angle of the "cow hock" breaks this straight line of bones and takes up the passing space, which forces the dog to "dust" or swing the passing leg in an arc around the supporting leg. Quite often these dogs will move wide behind, sometimes placing the back pads on the outside of both front pads rather than in line with them.

Weak hocks, ones with faulty bone assemblies, tend to bend outward when weight is applied to the leg. This is another condition that does not always show when the dog is standing at rest or in pose, when the legs are usually placed to favor this weakness.

The major cause in large dogs for "moving close" or "dusting" front and rear is a pendulum, rather than a flexed, swing of the legs. Some will swing their legs as though the only joints in them are the hip and shoulder sockets. (Where this is pronounced, you can even hear the toes rasp the covering of a show ring.) They will have trouble moving over rough ground and particularly through briars and tight ground covering. The weight-bearing leg reaches its maximum flexion at the midpoint of its arc of support, which will be directly under the center of the shoulder blade or the hip socket. The passing leg will go by at about this point and should be flexed considerably more. The dog should pick them up and then put them down.

A glaring fault in any dog is "crabbing," or moving with the back legs to one side of the front ones. One back leg may pass to the outside of the front while the other tries to split between them. This rear action is not in line with the front, nor even with the line of progress; thus, we have lost motion and energy. Also, the dog cannot turn quickly into the "crab."

Straight shoulders that shorten the fore-stride as well as overangulation and a lengthened back stride will create this condition, but the major cause is probably faulty timing of leg sequence.

In the slow walk, the dog should step off first with one front foot and then follow with the opposite back one. The front foot should be timed sufficiently ahead of the rear so that it is out of the way when the latter arrives. The eye can observe this in the walk and can check the difference in timing even though the back stride does not reach the vacated front pad mark. In the trot it is even more important that

242

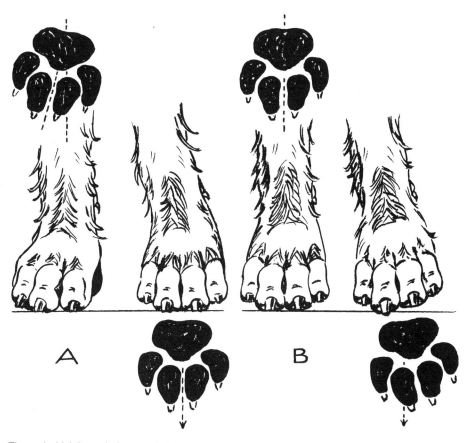

The pad which is angled outward 10 to 15 degrees, as in Fig. A, will, when swung inward under the center of gravity, be placed so that the action is off the two center toes, with the smaller toes used merely for balance on turns.

The pad that is directed straight ahead when the dog is standing as in Fig. B cannot be rotated when swung inward, so the action must come over one center toe, the smaller, outside toe providing less efficient action.

The outward turn of Fig. A is a rotation of the pastern rather than a bend, as in the "French Front," and is not to be confused with the latter.

the front action be ahead a split second of its coordinating back leg, or the advancing back leg will have no other choice but to sidestep.

In the fast gaits, front and back strides overlap. Half the arc of the stride is greater than half the length of the body, which in itself creates an overstride. Momentum also increases this condition.

Front and rear views of the dog probably show us more action fault than side views, but the latter show us the blending of forehand with rearhand for smooth, graceful passage. The foundation of gait is evident in the former two, and the beauty is revealed by the latter view. Two other important factors can be observed better from the side: the flexing of the legs and the supporting action of the pastern under weight, which latter is revealed by the bobbing rather than level movement of the withers.

Even though the trot is not the working gait of the Wolfhound, it is the best by which to judge his movement. All the faults and virtues of his ability to move will be reflected in the trot, and it is not so fast that the eye cannot see some of the virtues and faults. You can see enough to open the door on some of the things that you should look for in posture and to let you understand what to expect of the dog in the field.

Description of gait may sound like an exploration trip in search of faults, though it isn't intended as such. There is nothing more desirable than good movement in an animal and we cite faults for the same reason that traffic signs are posted—taking heed of them gives us a better ride and a quicker arrival at our destination.

As pointed out earlier, the Wolfhound's movement tells us a lot more about him than compliance to a simple paragraphic description of this single factor. All parts of his body and their cooperation enter into it. We may love that shaggy head and massive body as it stands majestically on our lawn like a statue sculptured by a great artist, but as the dog moves out across the field with powerful, flowing grace, he is at his best. There is far more beauty in the sweep of a gull over the waves than in his placid perch on the crown of a piling, and so it is with the flash of a Wolfhound in pursuit of game or running just for fun. The more we improve the movement of the Wolfhound, whether we take him afield or not, the better Wolfhound we will have—and that is the end toward which we strive.